COSMIC CHILD

COSMIC CHILD

INSPIRED WRITINGS
from the
THRESHOLD *of*
BIRTH

Selected and Arranged
by
EVE OLIVE

WRIGHTWOOD PRESS

CHICAGO

Wrightwood Press
PO Box 14702, Chicago, IL 60614-0702
www.wrightwoodpress.org

Cover Painting: "Geburt," by Ninetta Sombart, reproduced courtesy of Raffael-Verlag, Stockhornstrasse 5, Ittigen, Switzerland.

Cover design and book design by Maurice York.

Copyrighted poems in this volume are reprinted with permission. Since this page cannot legibly accommodate all the copyright notices, pages 163-169 constitute an extension of the copyright page.

NON-PROFITS, LIBRARIES, EDUCATIONAL INSTITUTIONS, WORKSHOP SPONSORS, STUDY GROUPS, ETC.
Special discounts and bulk purchases are available.
Please email sales@wrightwoodpress.org for more information.

ISBN   978-0-9801190-3-9

To the children of the world,
To those yet to come, and
To those who remember...

Our birth is but a sleep and a forgetting…

WILLIAM WORDSWORTH

Contents

Speaking of Angels

Meditations & Prayers

Postlude

Coda   151

Prelude

Prelude

IN 1979, WHEN MY HUSBAND AND I WERE EXPECTING OUR first grandchild, I wrote a series of seven poems which I called *Words for a Child* and sent them to our son and daughter-in-law in Australia. For months I had been meditating, inwardly accompanying this child on its way towards birth, so the poems all had a sense of pre-earthly awareness. As time went on, I realized there were other poems I knew of which have this sense of consciousness before birth. The fifth stanza of Wordsworth's *Ode: Intimations of Immortality from Recollections of Early Childhood*, which begins "Our birth is but a sleep and a forgetting," had inspired me since I first read it in high school. Then there was "The Vision" by Fiona Macleod, discovered some years later during my training in eurythmy—movement that brings speech to life. The poems of Louis MacNeice were a further discovery; later, came the fresh voice of Christy Barnes. Voices as far apart in time as Thomas Traherne and Langston Hughes, Rumi and Mary Oliver, began to assemble. Over a period of thirty-three years the collection gradually took form, and I would give it to friends who were expecting a child.

During the seventies, the work of Raymond Moody, Ph.D., M.D., on near death experiences was gaining attention. Of particular importance was his book *Life After Life*, published in 1975. At one end of life the veil was being pushed aside, but what about our entry into life – the great transition of birth? It appeared to me then that it was only the poets who had anything to offer. So, the little collection of poems seemed to have significance, and every now and then I would find and add another one. Within the last four or five years, however, I have become aware of a considerable number of books on the subject of consciousness of life before birth, such as *Babies Remember Birth* by David Chamberlain, Ph.D., and Elisabeth Hallett's *Stories of the Unborn Soul*. Others are mentioned in the "Books of Interest" at the end of this volume. Most of these books date from the early 1980s and on up into this 21st century. Maybe there is an evolution of consciousness at work here.

One day, when browsing in a bookstore, I found a little poem at the head of a chapter that I knew belonged in the collection. Later when I returned to the bookstore to search for it, I could not find the book or remember its name. All I could remember was the image in the poem, and that the name of the poet was Russian. That poem remained elusive for many years. The experience, however, made me realize that there were probably poems in every language that have this sense of a pre-birth state. Gradually such poems came to my attention through research and through friends who spoke other languages—first, two treasures in German, then one in Dutch. The collection now contains poems originally written in nine languages other than English. All are translated. The mysterious Russian poem that instigated this search finally came to light just three years ago. It is "The Angel," by Mikhail Lermontov. You will find it in the section "Speaking of Angels."

At the same time, often in the most serendipitous ways, more poems and stories in English began coming to my attention by poets both well-known and lesser-known. As I told friends about the collection, some would tell me of their own recollections of birth and of things their children had said when they were little, and so the whole section on "The Things Children Say" came into being. Little by little, the anthology took on its present form.

As the treasure trove of poems began to accumulate, the challenge of arranging them in a meaningful order arose. Should they be divided into *Voices—child's voice, mother's voice, father's voice?* By nationality or time period? In the end, it was the way in which a similar image might appear in two poems by different poets that led me to place certain poems side by side—that, and a sense of gradual movement from a pre-earthly state into the here and now that influenced the order.

This collection has grown organically over three decades—a long gestation period—and now it is time for it to be born. I hope it will find its way out into the world to delight and inspire many people, not only parents and parents-to-be. Ultimately it is a book for all of us, as we have each been through the great experience of birth, whether we remember it or not.

Eve Olive
Durham, North Carolina
September 2, 2012

Around the World across the Ages

Birth

Oh, fields of wonder
Out of which
Stars are born,
And moon and sun
And me as well,
Like stroke
Of lightning
In the night
Some mark
To make
Some word
To tell.

→ LANGSTON HUGHES
1902 – 1967

From Starry Realm

From starry realm
to green earth
I come

Dreaming through sphere
of planet and moon
I draw near

Falling asleep
to the home I have known
I awake
here on the earth

From the All
to the One
♪
fall

→ EVE OLIVE
1934 –

The Vision

In a fair place
　Of whin and grass,
　I heard feet pass
　Where no one was.

I saw a face
　Bloom like a flower—
　Nay, as the rainbow-shower
　Of a tempestuous hour.

It was not man, nor woman:
　It was not human:
　But, beautiful and wild
　Terribly undefiled,
　I knew an unborn child.

→ FIONA MACLEOD
1855 – 1905

Chorus of the Unborn

We the unborn:
Already longing starts to work on us,
The shores of blood widen in welcome,
And we sink into love like dew.
Yet time's shadows still lie like questions
Over our secret.

You lovers
Full of yearning,
And sick with farewell, listen:
It is we who begin to live in your glances,
In your hands that seek in the azure blue;
It is we who bear the fragrance of morning.
Already your breath is drawing us in,
Admitting us into the depths of your slumber,
Into your dreams, our kingdom on earth,
Where our black wet-nurse, the night,
Will let us grow
Until your eyes mirror us,
Until our voices speak in your ears.

Butterfly-like,
We are caught by the clasps of your longing—
And sold to the earth like the singing of birds—
Fragrant with morning,
We are lights that approach to illumine your sadness.

→ NELLY SACHS
1891 – 1970
Translated from the German
by Matthew Barton

Worldling

In a world of souls, I set out to find them.
They who first must find each other,
be each other's fate.
There, on the open road,
I gazed into each traveler's face.
Is it you? I would ask.
Are you the ones?
No, no, they said, or nothing at all.

How many cottages did I pass,
each with a mother, a father,
a firstborn, newly swaddled, crying;
or sitting in its little chair,
dipping a fat wooden spoon
into a steaming bowl,
its mother singing it a foolish song,
One, one, a lily's my care . . .

Through seasons I searched,
through years I can't remember,
reading the lichens and stones
as if one were marked
with my name, my face, my form.
By night and day I searched,
never sleeping, not wanting to fail,
not wanting to simply be a *star*.

Finally in a town like any other town,
in a house foursquare and shining,
its door wide open to the moon,
did I find them.

There, at the top of the winding stairs,
asleep in the big bed,
the sheets thrown off, curled
like question marks into each other's arms.

Past memory, I beheld them,
naked, their bodies without flaw.
It is I, I whispered.
I, the nameless one.
And my parents, spent by the dream
of creation, slept on.

➔ ELIZABETH SPIRES
1952 –

POEM

The spirit
  likes to dress up like this:
    ten fingers,
     ten toes,

shoulders, and all the rest
  at night
    in the black branches,
     in the morning

in the blue branches
  of the world.
    It could float, of course,
     but would rather

plumb rough matter.
  Airy and shapeless thing,
    it needs
     the metaphor of the body,

lime and appetite,
  the oceanic fluids;
    it needs the body's world,
     instinct

and imagination
  and the dark hug of time,
    sweetness
     and tangibility,

to be understood,
   to be more than pure light
      that burns
         where no one is—

so it enters us—
   in the morning
      shines from brute comfort
         like a stitch of lightning;

and at night
   lights up the deep and wondrous
      drownings of the body
         like a star.

→ MARY OLIVER
1935 –

To the Unborn

It might be in a cloud
Or the heart of a flower
    I see thee,
    My hand falls down
    Deprived of its power
    To depict thee.
A little face
Half crowned with glory,
Peeps o'er the rim of Heaven,
    Half afraid
Of the perilous pathway
    To the earth.
Then is my love too weak
To draw thee from the shadows?
And must thou wander forth,
Unfathered and unmothered
    With the stars?

➔ MARION CORNISH
1907 – 1972

Poem For Bella

An angel bright, a sun ray
At heaven's door did play
Watching, waiting patiently
For love to find its way.

→ MARIE SMITH
1951 –

Aubade for Infants

Snap the blind; I am not blind,
I must spy what stalks behind
Wall and window—Something large
Is barging up beyond the down,
Chirruping, hooting, hot of foot.

Beyond that wall what things befall?
My eye can fly though I must crawl.
Dance and dazzle—Something bright
Ignites the dumps of sodden cloud,
Loud and laughing, a fiery face…

Whose broad grimace (the voice is bass)
Makes nonsense of my time and place—
Maybe you think that I am young
I who flung before my birth
To mother earth the dawn-song too!

And you—
However old and deaf this year—
Were near me when that song was sung.

→ LOUIS MACNEICE
1907 − 1973

Made in Secret

They line up
little people yet to be.
Unborn faces in a crowd of futures.
None of them exist apart from a miracle
and yet how does that make them
so different from me?
They are all in halves right now.
A few dozen in her, determined.
Many millions inside of me
still fracturing in multitudes of possibilities
each one ready to collide with certainty
deciding a body
and framework of a personality.
The combinations could give forth one more
or maybe three
into full life and birth.

Yet now I can't help picturing them
all in a line waiting
in some shadowy star-shined
vestibule in space
pacing quietly, slowly
maybe hoping
praying
that we will seek them.
Already we have reached out
arms blind
taking and holding three

one that went in silence and mystery
two who have flourished like green shoots
as different as rose and sunflower
both lovely beneath the summer heat.
How daunting the task
of shedding all my sunlight for their nurture!
Can my garden
hold even these two blooms?
Yet how enticing the thought
of calling another bursting seed
across the boundary
of blood and flesh.

➔ VAN WAFFLE
1964 –

Conception

I wish to give us a child
Not just
an amalgam
of two kinds of genes,
random
in a sea of time.
But…
a wonder,
floating in the safe blue
of your womb.
Become,
Created,
in that moment,
that I was you
and you were me
and we found and met
the Other.

→ JAAP VAN DER WAL
1947 –
Translated from the Dutch
by Annelies Davidson

When Grapes Turn

When grapes
turn to wine,
they long for
our ability to change.

When stars
wheel around the North Pole,
they are longing for
our growing consciousness.

Wine got drunk
with us
not the other way.
The body developed
out of us,
not we from it.

We are bees,
and our body is a honeycomb.
We made
the body,
cell by cell
we made it.

→ RUMI
1207 – 1273
Translated from the Perisan
by Robert Bly

23

The Embryo

When the time comes for the embryo
to receive the spirit of life,
at that time the sun begins to help.
This embryo is brought into movement,
for the sun quickens it with spirit.

From the other stars this embryo
received only an impression,
until the sun shone upon it.
How did it become connected
with the shining sun
in the womb?

By ways hidden from our senses:
the way whereby gold is nourished,
the way a common stone becomes a garnet
and the ruby red,
the way fruit is ripened,
and the way courage comes
to one distraught
with fear.

→ RUMI
1207 – 1273
Translated from the Persian
by Kabir Helminski and Camille Helminski

Easter

The Mystery of Ephesus

World-engendered being, thou in a form of light,
By the Sun empowered, in the Moon's might,

Thou art endowed by Mars' creative ringing
And by Mercury's limb uplifted swinging,

Enlightened by Jupiter's wisdom streaming
And by Venus' love-bearing, beauty-beaming—

That Saturn's world-old spirit-inwardness
May consecrate thee to space's being and time's
      becoming.

→ RUDOLF STEINER
1861 – 1925
Translated from the German
by Ilse Kimball

Unsated Memory

Where is that world that I am fallen from?...
Ah, surely I was rather native there
Where all desires were lovely....

↷ LAURENCE BINYON
1869 – 1943

From Warmth of Darkness

From Warmth of Darkness
waiting
hovering
Knowing.

Half-way between a life
bathing in magenta
of a day's dawning
I AM
at one with Goodness, Love, and Mercy.

Choosing in Freedom
to say, "Yes!"

Leaving a world
of Oneness,
coming into
Light of Consciousness
separation
manifestation...
I AM.

Resting
timeless
in the upside down rainbow
Chalice of the Hierarchies'
Love
Descending
Spirit into Matter.

Cradle and hold me
tightly
Divine Sophia
Mother of all ways,
for the time is at hand.

How
did I get here?
A spark of Light — I AM
Oneness
in the heat of Love
opening to Grace.

➔ MARTHA LOVING ORGAIN

A Different Moon — Grave and Gay

The unborn child—
so long as it is growing in the mother's womb
its angel tells the story of its life,
and writes it into the body's becoming.

Overall in the form of its body
as eyes and ears develop,
the heart, the liver, the kidneys,
as the lines of the palm run their course,
so it is with the ten-fingered letters of each script
the angel writes, and thereby
the life of the child is written.

During the child's entire life span
the human within is occupied
in reading that which the angel, through
a duty-bound calling, gathered up and wrote down.

Whereupon, day after day, the human
being true or false, writes the life's
unfolding solution in earthly life, as he will.
That is the new.
Yet the blessing of the new
he receives from the well
out of which all life springs.

Deeply penetrating is the life stream
–that which the newborn encounters
is more penetrating than the sunrise thereafter.
But deepest of all, the light imprints

speech into the human being,
for light sparks the spirit's first torch.

All about this then is a shout of joy
in those first uttered, awakened words.
Then jubilation—breaking forth as the spring,
and with countless fountains flowing uniting in a
    stream—
has wafted a wordy language, overladen with sense.

And who then remembers the fountain of
    jubilation?

➔ ALFRED BAUR
1925 – 2008
Translated from the German
by Elaine Maria Upton

The Old Man's Idyll

The voice of a one year old

What does he say? Is he speaking, think you? I do
　　believe so.
But to whom does he speak? To someone in the heavens;
To those whom we call spirits; to heaven's heights,
To the gentle beating of the invisible wing that passes,
To the shadows, to the wind, perchance to the young
　　brother passed away.
The child brings with him some small morsel of the
　　heaven he has left.
He descends unaware, to the welcome of man.
He trembles in the manner of grass, of leaves.
The babble of the child comes before language, as the
　　flower
Comes before the fruit, the former more beautiful, the
　　latter better,
If indeed it is better to be more necessary.
The guileless child at the threshold of human woes
Contemplates this strange, foreboding place,
Cannot comprehend, is amazed, and not seeing God,
His voice falters, humble, confiding, pathetic;
But weeping is followed by singing;
His first words, like his first footsteps are fearful.
Then hope is born…

O divine chiaroscuro: the language of the child!
The child, who seems able to disempower destiny;
The child, who unwittingly teaches us Nature;
His rosy mouth is the wondrous orifice,
From which falls, O majesty of the frail and unadorned,

Into the unrecognized abyss the unknown Word.
Innocence is amongst us, with such generosity!
Such a great gift from heaven! Who can know what sage
    advice,
What blaze of kindness, what faith and love
Are poured by the souls of children through their
    flickering twilight,
In the midst of the bitter and sinister quarrel that
    afflicts us,
Onto the souls of men?
Can one pierce the depths of this language, where one
    senses
The passage of all that sets the innocent a-tremble.
No. Men are moved and listen to this confusion
Of syllables that fly into the wonder of the dawn,
A language tinged with the sky's inflection;
But they do not understand and walk away with their
    own words;
It was nothing; a breath of air, an exhalation, a murmur;
The word is not complete when the soul is unready—

What do you know of this? This cry, this song from out a
    nest
Begins with man and is completed by the angel.

→ VICTOR HUGO
1802 – 1885
Translated from the French
by Geoffrey Vitale

To My Son

You dozed without destiny in blue eternity
where no time and no thought shot
its shining road, from blissful dreaming moons
a gentle-eyed silvershine floated out in space.
It wasn't night, oppressed by memory of life,
but more the first glimmer of the morning
in all a peace of eternity like swaddled ribbons
and cool sheets about you, desired son.

A whirring arose, like a flock of migratory birds
hovering about and over all oceans of eternity,
but you lay light as a lily on blue waves
that goddesses of dreams guided in and out
like a waterlily swayed by sleeping hours of night
and laid your fairy cheek in gentle rest
in the lap of the wave, while a ray of light
wrought by heavenly shaping stood by your resting place.

But I went daydreaming in my dales
where waterfalls and steep mountains built me into a man.
O heaven of youth! Sunwarm, sunwarm it moves
along the ridge by burning breast-fire.
And the spring of love untied all ribbons,
I felt like swimming up in song
and mist of sun along all mountains and peaks
while time rolled into eternity...

And the longing rowed out of its fjords
and learned the long waves rolling
and raised its voice, like distant thunder,
until your dreams of home lit up.
Then ethereal spiritlightened circles broke
and the earth reached you with its power of gravity.
Then you hovered every moment in lessening circles
until you lay warm cheeked within your cradle.

→ OLAV NYGAARD
1884 – 1924
Translated from old Norwegian
by Lilleberta Sandved and Holger Nygard

May You Have Life

May you have life
from our first meeting
grow from our earth of love

You will be beautiful
like the morning
if life finds you in our first night
beautiful like the first morning.

Your face
will be like the light
and night will lend its fragrance to your hair.

Who can believe that you
are our daughter?
Your eyes hide the brilliance
of the North Star.
Your feet will be quick
like all the thoughts we have sent
across the sea.

It will be strange to see you
like a child
among other children.

→ MARIE TAKVAM
1926 – 2008
Translated from the Norwegian
by Lilleberta Sandved and Holger Nygard

Wonder

How like an Angel came I down!
How bright are all things here!
When first among his Works I did appear
O how their Glory did me crown!
The World resembled his ETERNITY,
In which my Soul did walk;
And evr'y thing that I did see
Did with me talk.

The Skies in their Magnificence,
The lovely lively Air,
Oh how divine, how soft, how sweet, how fair!
The Stars did entertain my Sense;
And all the Works of God so bright and pure,
So rich and great, did seem,
As if they ever must endure
In my Esteem.

A Native Health and Innocence
Within my Bones did grow,
And while my God did all his Glories show
I felt a vigor in my Sense
That was all Spirit: I within did flow
With Seas of Life like Wine;
I nothing in the World did know
But 'twas Divine.

Harsh rugged Objects were conceal'd,
    Oppressions, Tears and Cries,
Sins, Griefs, Complaints, Dissentions, weeping Eyes,
    Were hid: And only things reveal'd
Which heavenly Spirits and the Angels prize:
    The State of Innocence
    And Bliss, not Trades and Poverties,
        Did fill my Sense.

The Streets seem'd paved with golden Stones,
    The Boys and Girls all mine;
To me how did their lovely faces shine!
    The Sons of men all Holy ones,
In Joy and Beauty, then appear'd to me;
    And ev'ry thing I found
    (While like an Angel I did see)
        Adorn'd the Ground.

Rich Diamonds, and Pearl, and Gold
    Might ev'ry where be seen;
Rare Colors, yellow, blue, red, white, and green
    Mine Eyes on ev'ry side behold:
All that I saw, a Wonder did appear,
    Amazement was my Bliss:
    That and my Wealth met ev'ry where.
        No joy to this!

Curs'd, ill-devis'd Proprieties
    With Envy, Avarice,
And Fraud, (those Fiends that spoil ev'n Paradise)
    Were not the Object of mine Eyes;

Nor Hedges, Ditches, Limits, narrow Bounds:
    I dreamt not ought of those,
  But in surveying all men's Grounds
    I found Repose.

For Property its self was mine,
    And Hedges, Ornaments:
Walls, Houses, Coffers, and their rich Contents,
    To make me Rich combine.
Clothes, costly Jewels, Laces, I esteem'd
    My Wealth by others worn,
  For me they all to wear them seem'd,
    When I was born.

→ THOMAS TRAHERNE
1637 – 1674

The Salutation

These little limbs,
  These eyes and hands which here I find,
These rosy cheeks wherewith my life begins;
  Where have ye been? Behind
What curtain were ye from me hid so long?
Where was, in what abyss, my speaking tongue? ...

  When silent I
  So many thousand, thousand Years
Beneath the dust did in a Chaos lie,
  How could I Smiles or Tears,
Or Lips or Hands or Eyes or Ears perceive?
Welcome ye Treasures which I now receive.

  I that so long
  Was nothing from eternity,
Did little think such joys as ear or tongue
  To celebrate or see:
Such sounds to hear, such hands to feel, such feet,
Beneath the skies on such a ground to meet.

  New Burnished joys,
  Which yellow gold and pearls excel!
Such sacred treasures are the limbs in boys,
  In which a soul doth dwell;
Their organizèd joints and azure veins
More wealth include than all the world contains.

From Dust I rise,
  And out of Nothing now awake;
These brighter Regions which salute mine Eyes,
  A Gift from God I take:
The Earth, the Seas, the Light, the day, the lofty Skies,
The Sun and Stars are mine; if those I prize.

Long time before
  I in my mother's womb was born,
A God, preparing, did this glorious store,
  The world, for me adorn.
Into this Eden so divine and fair,
So wide and bright, I come His son and heir.

A Stranger here
  Strange things doth meet, strange Glory see,
Strange Treasures lodg'd in this fair World appear,
  Strange all and New to me:
But that they mine should be who Nothing was,
That Strangest is of all; yet brought to pass.

→ THOMAS TRAHERNE
1637 – 1674

Meeting

Whither prideful sails that majesty of clouds
Powerful and delicate in their delirious chaos
Migrating whither, to what star-pierced heaven?
Below, the snow proffers the Night
Her sparkling mirror
Brightening the deep blues of the mysteries.
O fathomless tenderness
Whose serenity
Brings me peace and lights up my heart.

What are those kindly processions
Of angelic wings that take their leave?
They seem to carry cradles or cribs
Of souls awaiting their coming births.
Ah! How sacred is the warmth of such tenderness!

Seven years had passed.
When in front of the class
Where every gaze, mingles with mine,
And artless offers me the single beaker of each thirst

I recognized, with such emotion,
O tenderness, setting, memories—
So real and vibrant
Those gentle presences who from the Holy Night
Came down anew to join us.

> → HÉLÈNE BESNARD
> *1952 –*
> *Translated from the French*
> *by Geoffrey Vitale*

This Island

How did we come to land here,
for what purpose... from where...?
is that strange vessel still there on the shore?
and if the anchor has been weighed,
to where... to where...?

Hush, close the doors...
love one another...

➔ ADRIAAN ROLAND HOLST
1888 – 1976
Translated from the Dutch
by Else Göttkens

The Little Children Know

How it appears in eternal joy
    In heaven, on high, above,
The children, the little ones alone, know,
    They come, yes directly from above.

But they, little and dumbfounded, cannot say it.
    They must withhold it meanwhile:
And they grow near you and chat with you
      acceptably.
    Then, eternity, sadly, they forget.

→ ROBERT HAMERLING
1830 – 1889
Translated from the German
by Elaine Maria Upton

Ode: Intimations of Immortality from
Recollections of Early Childhood

The Child is father of the Man;
And I could wish my days to be
Bound each to each by natural piety.

I

There was a time when meadow, grove, and
    stream,
The earth, and every common sight,
        To me did seem
        Apparelled in celestial light.
The glory and the freshness of a dream.
It is not now as it hath been of yore;-
        Turn whereso'er I may,
        By night or day,
The things which I have seen I now can see no
    more.

...

V

Our birth is but a sleep and a forgetting:
The Soul that rises with us, our life's Star,
        Hath had elsewhere its setting,
        And cometh from afar:
        Not in entire forgetfulness,
        And not in utter nakedness,
But trailing clouds of glory do we come
        From God, who is our home:

Heaven lies about us in our infancy!
Shades of the prison-house begin to close
    Upon the growing Boy,
But he beholds the light, and whence it flows
    He sees it in his joy;
The Youth, who daily farther from the east
    Must travel, still is Nature's Priest,
    And by the vision splendid
    Is on his way attended;
At length the Man perceives it die away,
And fade into the light of common day.

→ WILLIAM WORDSWORTH
1770 – 1850

I Think Continually of Those

I think continually of those who were truly great.
Who, from the womb, remembered the soul's history
Through corridors of light where the hours are suns,
Endless and singing. Whose lovely ambition
Was that their lips, still touched with fire,
Should tell of the spirit clothed from head to foot in song.
And who hoarded from the spring branches
The desires falling across their bodies like blossoms.

What is precious is never to forget
The essential delight of the blood drawn from ageless
        springs
Breaking through rocks in worlds before our earth;
Never to deny its pleasure in the simple morning light,
Nor its grave evening demand for love;
Never to allow gradually the traffic to smother
With noise and fog, the flowering of the spirit.

Near the snow, near the sun, in the highest fields
See how these names are fêted by the waving grass,
And by the streamers of white cloud,
And whispers of wind in the listening sky.
The names of those who in their lives fought for life,
Who wore at their hearts the fire's centre.
Born of the sun, they travelled a short while towards the
        sun,
And left the vivid air signed with their honour.

→ STEPHEN SPENDER
1909 − 1995

46

The Summer of Celia

Is this a dream? The August sun,
the trees in the moment before their decline,

the high bodiless clouds skimming the horizon,
the water a second skin my strokes

slough off, and Celia swimming
her small strokes inside me as I swim?

Celia, the first and only one,
who fits like a seed in my sleeping palm,

who comes unspeaking to me in dreams,
her eyes half blue, half brown.

I cannot remember my own time, floating
in the warm birth sac, my mother asleep,

the waters still, the two of us dreaming.
What, what did we dream of?

Speak to me, Celia. Speak. Speak.
Before birth erases memory and suddenly

you are taken from me, then given back,
wrapped in the white gown of forgetting,

changed, utterly changed. As I will be.
This is our summer, the summer of the dream

we will, too soon, awaken from,
shocked and surprised, in our separate bodies.

➔ ELIZABETH SPIRES
1952 –

Threshold

Well I remember
  her holding me, rocking me
 awash in her soft silent
    darkness and sound

Before I was born
  I breathed in her water
 salt on my skin
    my body becoming

A child I felt
  breathed in me too
 well I remember
    crying out Mama

At the last threshold
  I will step from the shore
 to that same reservoir
    home of all waters

➜ PATTI TANA

Seven Seas

Chanteys for you, daughter,
your childhood songs, sung on winter evenings
and long car journeys, songs of effort

and departure, rough as rope,
hauling out of the body a desire
older than the desire to give in

to bone-weariness and sleep.
"Go down, you blood red roses,
go down," down to whatever drives

the heart to beat, eyes
to blink against salt and glare,
and make it answer. The child

in the womb grows to the heartbeat
of her mother, hears her singing
faraway, calling to her, across oceans
of shared salt and blood.

→ MAURA HIGH

Celia Dreaming

Bright sphere, I have watched you dreaming,
your face a wordless whorl, an inward-folding flower
whose petals spiral round a dream of milk and hunger,
a fear of falling farther than outstretched arms
can catch you, while I stand beyond the circle
of your dreaming joy and fear, amazed
that you have been here half a year. Half a year!

Yesterday in the garden as you slept on my shoulder,
I watched a bee tunnel into the Rose of Sharon,
summer's late-blooming flower, watched its head,
then furred legs, disappear completely
into the heart of the flower, back beyond
the body's origin, as if it could be unborn.
Sphere, before you were with me, where were you?

Waking, you reached to touch the white face
of the flower, then another, and another, faces
quickly flowing past us, or held and stared into,
as if between two hands, the way a countenance
that lies in rippling water finally comes clear,
making me wonder how of all the million millions
it is you, you who are with me, you and not another.

→ ELIZABETH SPIRES
1952 –

50

One for Lily on Her First Birthday

One is an I
upright and bouncing
between earth and heaven.

Is a number that contains multitudes,
counting backward to before
you were born,
when you were desired merely:
zeroes upon zeroes, roots and powers,
Ys and Xs, accumulating
can I say, by chance?
The Master asks,
What body did you have then?
One before it was written,
the pencil poised over the paper.
The genie before it billows
from the tarnished lamp.
The glassblower's breath
before it bubbles
in the twirling glass.

One stands alone for the first time,
one totters round the table,
one tumbles and springs,
one hoots for joy.

→ MAURA HIGH

The Beginning

'Where have I come from, where did you discover me?'
the baby asked its mother. She answered, half crying,
half laughing, and clasping the baby to her breast,
'You were hidden in my heart as its desire, my darling.
You were in the dolls of my childhood's games.
When in girlhood my heart was opening its petals,
you hovered as a fragrance about it.
In all my hopes and my loves, in my life,
in the life of my mother you have lived.

You have floated down the stream of the world's life,
and at last you have stranded on my heart.
As I gaze on your face, mystery overwhelms me;
you who belong to all have become mine.
For fear of losing you I hold you tight to my breast.
What magic has snared the world's treasure
in these slender arms of mine?'

→ RABINDRANATH TAGORE
1861 – 1941

Song

Where did you come from, baby dear?
Out of the everywhere into here.

Where did you get those eyes so blue?
Out of the sky as I came through.

What makes the light in them sparkle and spin?
Some of the starry twinkles left in.

Where did you get that little tear?
I found it waiting when I got here.

What makes your forehead so smooth and high?
A soft hand stroked it as I went by.

What makes your cheek like a warm white rose?
I saw something better than any one knows.

Whence that three-cornered smile of bliss?
Three angels gave me at once a kiss.

Where did you get this pearly ear?
God spoke, and it came out to hear.

Where did you get those arms and hands?
Love made itself into bonds and bands.

Feet, whence did you come, you darling things?
From the same box as the cherubs' wings.

How did they all just come to be you?
God thought about me, and so I grew.

But how did you come to us, you dear?
God thought about you, and so I am here.

→ GEORGE MACDONALD
1824 – 1905

53

Bumble-Baby

My baby's like a bumblebee,
So round and good with fuzzy head
And tiny legs all tucked in bed,
And she sleeps so busily!

In her dreams, with cozy love,
She hums and hovers just above
Her little body through the sunny
Fields she roamed before her birth;
Sucks and harvests heaven's honey,
Hoards it home for hives on earth.

When she wakes, she looks up through
Eyes like pansy-petal dew;
Her cheeks and breath are flowers too.
Tell me, baby, what are you?
A tiny blossom-bundle, maybe?
A bee-flower? Or a bumble-baby!

➜ CHRISTY BARNES
1909 – 2002

54

Mother's Song to a Baby

First
this little baby
has been given life
through the medicine man's song
through the medicine man's prayer
for this baby the songs
have been sung

Next
the baby's mother
has taken care of him
with songs of the rain gods

This
little baby
in his cloud-cradle
was watched over
by his mother

It
was nice
how the clouds
came up like foam
and
as if he
was among them
this little baby
was cared for

→ NATIVE AMERICAN

My Sun!

My sun!
My morning star!
Help this child to become a man.
I name him
Rain-dew Falling!
I name him
Star Mountain!

➜ TEWA PRAYER

Baby's World

I wish I could take a quiet corner in the heart of my baby's very own world.

I know it has stars that talk to him, and a sky that stoops down to his face to amuse him with its silly clouds and rainbows.

Those who make believe to be dumb, and look as if they never could move, come creeping to his window with their stories and with trays crowded with bright toys.

I wish I could travel by the road that crosses baby's mind, and out beyond all bounds;

Where messengers run errands for no cause between the kingdoms of kings of no history;

Where Reason makes kites of her laws and flies them, and Truth sets Fact free from its fetters.

→ RABINDRANATH TAGORE
1861 – 1941

rumors

what could the clouds be
whispering about me?
they don't even know my name

hush child!
hush

ain't i told you a thousand
times to whisper when we
walking thru the sky.

girl, cloud know your name
moon too
stars told 'em

they know 'bout you
know 'bout you before you were ever born

→ JAKI SHELTON GREEN
1953 −

Sacred Texts and Sayings

And Adam said to Eve, "Look at thine eyes, and at mine, which afore beheld angels in heaven, praising; and they, too, without ceasing.

"But now we do not see as we did: our eyes have become of flesh; they cannot see in like manner as they saw before."

THE FIRST BOOK OF ADAM AND EVE 4:8,9
The Forgotten Books of Eden

...

Before I formed you in the womb I knew you, and before you were born I consecrated you.

JEREMIAH 1:5
The Bible NRSV

...

He it is Who shapes you in the womb as He wills.
There is no Deity save Him, the Almighty, the Truly Wise.

QUR'AN 3:6

...

When forty-two nights have passed over the drop,
God sends an angel to it, who shapes it and makes it
ears, eyes, skin, flesh and bones.
Then he says, "O Lord, is it male or female?"
And your Lord decides what He wishes.

Hadith (SAYING) ATTRIBUTED TO
THE PROPHET MUHAMMAD,
FROM THE *Hadith* COLLECTION OF SALIH MUSLIM

Domine, probasti

For you yourself created my innermost parts; you knit me together in my mother's womb.

I will thank you because I am marvelously made: your works are wonderful, and I know it well.

My body was not hidden from you, while I was being made in secret and woven in the depths of the earth.

Your eyes beheld my limbs, yet unfinished in the womb; all of them were written in your book; they were fashioned day by day, when as yet there were none of them.

PSALM 139: 12-15
The Book of Common Prayer according to the use of
The Episcopal Church, 1979

...

And Mary arose in those days, and went into the hill country with haste, into a city of Ju'da;

And entered into the house of Zăch'ă-ri'ăs, and saluted Elisabeth.

And it came to pass, that, when Elisabeth heard the salutation of Mary, the babe leaped in her womb; and Elisabeth was filled with the Holy Ghost:

And she spake out with a loud voice, and said, Blessed art thou among women, and blessed is the fruit of thy womb.

And whence is this to me that the mother of my Lord should come to me?

For lo, as soon as the voice of thy salutation sounded in mine ears, the babe leaped in my womb for joy.

LUKE 1:39-44
The Bible KJV

Jesus said, "If they say to you, 'Where have you come from?' say to them, 'We have come from the light, from the place where the light came into being, established [itself], and appeared in their image.' If they say to you, 'Is it you?' say, 'We are its children, and we are the chosen of the living father.'

If they ask you, 'What is the evidence of your Father in you?' say to them, 'It is motion and rest.'"

THE GOSPEL OF THOMAS 50:1-3

. . .

I came forth from the Father, and am come into the world: again, I leave the world, and go to the Father.

JOHN 16:28
The Bible KJV

. . .

> From Delight we came into existence,
> In Delight we grow.
> At the end of our journey's close,
> Into Delight we retire.

From the Upanishads

. . .

According to the Buddha there are four modes of birth, each apparently the result of the degree of awareness achieved in previous lives:

"Brethren, in this world, one comes into existence in the mother's womb without knowing, stays in it without knowing, and comes out from the mother's womb without knowing; this is the first.

Brethren, one comes into existence in the mother's womb knowingly, stays in it without knowing, and comes out from it without knowing; this is the second.

Brethren, one comes into existence in the mother's womb knowingly, stays in it knowingly, and comes out from it without knowing; this is the third.

Brethren, in this world one comes into existence in the mother's womb knowingly, stays in it knowingly, and comes out from it knowingly; this is the fourth."

GAUTAMA BUDDHA
from the Sangiti Sutta

. . .

If our clothes are worn out
    we put aside our old ones,
And in their place
    we put on new ones.
In old age we rest
    after life's exhausting struggle,
Leaving in the grave
    the earthly garment of our body.
Until nature has once again
    made us a bodily sheath,

A new garment,
  lovingly prepared in our mother's womb.
And when we awaken again,
  there shines in golden splendor
The youthfully radiant day,
  which arose before us as a miracle.

from the Bhagavad Gita

...

I am Today.
I am Yesterday.
I am Tomorrow.
Moving through repeated births I remain
  strong and young...
See, I fly like a bird,
And floating in the air I descend to earth...
Stepping forth I follow the tracks
  of my previous deeds; for I am
A child of Yesterday,
My becoming is in the keeping of the gods
  of Akeru.

from the Egyptian Book of the Dead

Know, O Beloved

Know, O beloved, that we are not created
in jest or at random
but marvelously made
and for some great end.

→ AL-GHAZALI
1058 – 1111
Translated from the Persian
by Claud Field

Christ is Born

Christ is born,
Quickening memory:
From the womb
Of spirit powers
We have our being.

→ ROGER SCHULTZ

For a Newborn Child

For B. v. Z

The stone that slumbers in the earth,
The dreaming blossom on the bough,
The birds and rabbits in the wood,
The busy bee, the patient cow;
The lion, leaping fierce and bold,
The soaring eagle in the height,
The snow-white lambkin in the fold,
All the great, wide, sun-lit world
Give you greeting, baby bright,
Wish you wisdom, power, joy,
     You tiny, infant boy!

The ways of this great earth
Are wise and beautiful —
Albeit rough and long.
The ways of man are mighty, gloriful —
Though heaped with wrong;
Wrought of woe and wonder,
Of suffering and song,
Ways of knowledge, love and hope,
Hammered in the heart's clear heat.
For long ago a star-bright baby
Trod the earth with tender feet,
Held within His heart the Sun —
The bright, all-gracious, mighty One —

Walked the ways of death and night
To wake the world with living Light.
And now the heavenly host on high,
And all things that live and die,
Praise His Name and mortal birth —
And He walks with every child
    Who comes upon the earth.

→ ARVIA MACKAYE EGE
1925 − 2011

Like Every Newborn

"The Lord is King, and hath put on glorious
apparel; the Lord hath put on his apparel
and girded himself with strength."

Like every newborn, he has come from very far.
His eyes are closed against the brilliance of the star.
So glorious is he, he goes to this immoderate length
To show his love for us, discarding power and strength.
Girded for war, humility his mighty dress,
He moves into the battle wholly weaponless.

→ MADELEINE L'ENGLE
1918 – 2007

The Risk of Birth, Christmas, 1973

This is no time for a child to be born,
With the earth betrayed by war & hate
And a comet slashing the sky to warn
That time runs out & the sun burns late.

That was no time for a child to be born,
In a land in the crushing grip of Rome;
Honour & truth were trampled by scorn—
Yet here did the Savior make his home.

When is the time for love to be born?
The inn is full on the planet earth,
And by a comet the sky is torn—
Yet Love still takes the risk of birth.

> ⇥ MADELEINE L'ENGLE
> *1918 – 2007*

How Did I Separate
Myself from Your Thrall

How did I separate myself from Your thrall
and again dive low into the deep,
and again descend into darkness' lap,
if not there also Your very being did call
to that Spirit light in which I also receive life's might,
as though a butterfly weaving in light?
How, unless to me was gifted the task
to descend and suffer death at last?

How could I separate myself from such a place
where every last dream is fulfilled,
and unspeakable suffering makes no hardened face,
but rather, there I am only by Heaven sealed?
And except that what remains is longing's thorn,
how could I now with passion go from You there —
how, except to love You more, in that world where
they do not yet see You as the Sun?

Out of love, so forcefully sent from You
from Heaven to Earth, I know:
only always and again I am filled by You,
and joyfully I bear such departure, so
that You must reveal Yourself as a Well to me,
one that without ceasing nourishes me.
Now I can also follow you readily
to hell, for Your Heaven creates me young eternally.

→ CHRISTIAN MORGENSTERN
1871 – 1914
Translated from the German
by Elaine Maria Upton

Prayer before Birth

I am not yet born; O hear me.
Let not the bloodsucking bat or the rat or the stoat or the
   club-footed ghoul come near me.

I am not yet born, console me.
I fear that the human race may with tall walls wall me,
   with strong drugs dope me, with wise lies lure me,
     on black racks rack me, in blood-baths roll me.

I am not yet born; provide me
With water to dandle me, grass to grow for me, trees to talk
   to me, sky to sing to me, birds and a white light
     in the back of my mind to guide me.

I am not yet born; forgive me
For the sins that in me the world shall commit, my words
   when they speak me, my thoughts when they think me,
     my treason engendered by traitors beyond me,
       my life when they murder by means of my
         hands, my death when they live me.

I am not yet born; rehearse me
In the parts I must play and the cues I must take when
   old men lecture me, bureaucrats hector me, mountains
     frown at me, lovers laugh at me, the white
       waves call me to folly and the desert calls
         me to doom and the beggar refuses
           my gift and my children curse me.

I am not yet born; O hear me,
Let not the man who is beast or who thinks he is God
   come near me.

I am not yet born; O fill me
With strength against those who would freeze my
   humanity, would dragoon me into a lethal automaton,
    would make me a cog in a machine, a thing with
     one face, a thing, and against all those
      who would dissipate my entirety, would
       blow me like thistledown hither and
        thither or hither and thither
         like water held in the
          hands would spill me.

Let them not make me a stone and let them not spill me.
Otherwise kill me.

→ LOUIS MACNEICE
1907 – 1963

Unborn Child

From the radiant one,
The sun,
Through the rainbow
Down the sky
I came with flower
And butterfly,
But blossomed not
Upon the earth—
Slipped all at once
Through death and birth
And budded back
Into the glow
And colors of the shining bow,
Building of its light
A home
Up from your hearts
To heaven's dome.

Tend and rock me
Where I lie
In the vastness of the sky.
Where your quiet souls are wed,
Tuck up and watch
My starry bed
Till your two hearts cradle me
In their beating
Lovingly.

→ CHRISTY BARNES
1909 – 2002

73

The Almond Tree

Jonathan: 1965

I

All the way to the hospital
The lights were green as peppermints.
Trees of black iron broke into leaf
ahead of me, as if
I were the lucky prince
in an enchanted wood
summoning summer with my whistle,
banishing winter with a nod.
Swung by the road from bend to bend,
I was aware that blood was running
down through the delta of my wrist
and under arches
of bright bone. Centuries,
continents it had crossed;
from an undisclosed beginning
spiraling to an unmapped end.

II

Crossing (at sixty) Magdalen Bridge
Let it be a son, a son, said
the man in the driving mirror,
Let it be a son. The tower
held up its hand: the college
bells shook their blessings on his head.

III

I parked in an almond's
shadow blossom, for the tree
was waving, waving me
upstairs with a child's hands.

IV

Up
the spinal stair
and at the top
along
a bone-white corridor
the blood tide swung
me swung me to a room
whose walls shuddered
with the shuddering womb.
Under the sheet
wave after wave, wave
after wave beat
on the bone coast, bringing
ashore – whom?
        New –
minted, my bright farthing!
Coined by our love, stamped with
our images, how you
enrich us! Both
you make one. Welcome
to your white sheet,
my best poem!

V

At seven-thirty
the visitors' bell
scissored the calm
of the corridors.
The doctor walked with me
to the slicing doors.
His hand upon my arm,
his voice – *I have to tell
you* – set another bell
beating in my head:
your son is a mongol
the doctor said.

VI

How easily the word went in –
clean as a bullet
leaving no mark on the skin,
stopping the heart within it.
This was my first death.
The 'I' ascending on a slow
last thermal breath
studied the man below
as a pilot treading air might
the buckled shell of his plane –
boot, glove and helmet
feeling no pain
from the snapped wires' radiant ends.
Looking down from a thousand feet
I held four walls in the lens

of an eye; wall, window, the street
a torrent of windscreens, my own
car under its almond tree,
and the almond waving me down.
I wrestled against gravity,
but light was melting and the gulf
cracked open. Unfamiliar
the body of my late self
I carried to the car.

VII

The hospital – its heavy freight
lashed down ship-shape ward over ward –
steamed into night with some on board
soon to be lost if the desperate
charts were known. Others would come
altered to land or find the land
altered. At their voyage's end
some would be added to, some
diminished. In a numbered cot
my son sailed from me; never to come
ashore into my kingdom
speaking my language. Better not
look that way. The almond tree
was beautiful in labour. Blood –
dark, quickening, bud after bud
split, flower after flower shook free.
On the darkening wind a pale
face floated. Out of reach. Only when
the buds, all the buds were broken

77

would the tree be in full sail.
In labour the tree was becoming
itself. I, too, rooted in earth
and ringed by darkness, from the death
of myself saw myself blossoming,
wrenched from the caul of my thirty
years' growing, fathered by my son,
unkindly in a kind season
by love shattered and set free.

→ JON STALLWORTHY
1935 –

Firstborn

You turn to the window for the first time.
I am called to the cot
to see your focus shift,
take tendril-hold on a shaft
of sun, explore its dusty surface, climb
to an eye you cannot

meet. You have a sickness they cannot heal,
the doctors say: locked in
your body you will remain.
Well, I have been locked in mine.
We will tunnel each other out. You seal
the covenant with a grin.

In the days we have known one another,
my little mongol love,
I have learnt more from your lips
than you will from mine perhaps:
I have learnt that to live is to suffer,
to suffer is to live.

→ JON STALLWORTHY
1935 –

War Baby

He has not even seen you, he
Who gave you your mortality;
And you, so small, how can you guess
His courage or his loveliness?

Yet in my quiet mind I pray
He passed you on the darkling way—
His death, your birth, so much the same—
And holding you, breathed once your name.

→ PAMELA HOLMES
1922 – 2002

Near Death
A sonnet for Aaron Kramer, 1997

"Do not go gentle?" Dylan missed the mark;
as if we all must think of death as dark.
I think that death's more gentle than a birth.
I've seen a light that glows beyond the earth;
but not a heaven, not Elysian Fields.
One needn't find salvation; rather, yield
to that same light that little children miss
in nurseries where doting parents kiss
their fears away indulgently. But why?
Suppose it isn't fear that makes kids cry
but yearning for the pre-birth light they left.
Then go, good journeyman, gently cleft.
Greet death as quietly as candles burn.
From light you came. To light you shall return.

→ DAVID B. AXELROD
1943 —

I Watched

I watched
as the baby watched

Are you looking at the different shapes
her mother asked
but mother could not see her eyes
as she held her

I could see her eyes
ancient, venerable eyes
serious eyes
in a six-week-old body
eyes that watched, looked
not at our physical world
but at something we could not see

What was it she could see
in this long slow meditative gazing
this absorbed looking
this infinite gaze
What was this being in this tiny form
            experiencing

Was it the sadness
of saying goodbye
            to something
            to somewhere
We could not see
even as we celebrated
her advent upon the earth

→ EVE OLIVE
  1934 –

Into My Childhood Days

Into my childhood days shone the loveliness
Of the Kingdom before birth
In a dream light that knew no death.
Now at the end of my life
Rays from the farther shore
Reveal the immortality of all things mortal.

→ ELEANOR TRIVES
1892 – 1975

The Breeze at Dawn

The breeze at dawn has secrets to tell you.
Don't go back to sleep.
You must ask for what you really want.
Don't go back to sleep.
People are moving back and forth across the doorsill
where the two worlds touch.
The door is round and open.
Don't go back to sleep.

→ RUMI
1207–1273
Translated from the Persian
by Coleman Barks

Primeval Self

Primeval self
From whom all things derive,
Primeval self
To whom all things return,
Primeval self
That in me lives—
To thee will I aspire.

➜ FROM THE UPANISHADS

Life After Death

Life after death—
Life before birth;
Only by knowing both
Do we know eternity.

→ RUDOLF STEINER
1861-1925
Translated from the German
by Margot M. Saar

The
Things
Children
Say

Consciousness before Birth

Phoebe

MY WIFE AND I were sitting up in bed one morning playing with our rather precocious two year old when I asked her:

"Tell me, Phoebe, what made you want to come to mommy and me and be our little girl?"

Without hesitation, she answered:

"Well I just flew by to look, but you closed the windows and pulled off my wings."

MARK HULBERT

Jane

WHEN SHE WAS ABOUT SEVEN YEARS OLD, my daughter said to me that I hadn't wanted her, had I? "But of course I did!" I replied.

"No you didn't mummy, not when I was first in your tummy; you were very unhappy. I sang and sang to you but you would not listen and one day you did and then everything was all right."

Jane was quite correct. I was 40 when she was born and at first I was very unhappy to find myself pregnant, but after a few weeks the anticipation and excitement took hold of me and I longed to meet this new little life, and after she was born

I was very careful never to tell her that I had been unhappy at first. Jane doesn't remember this conversation now but I hold it in my heart.

JANET PARSONS

Karen

MY THREE-YEAR-OLD NIECE, Karen, was particularly fond of my husband. "Brucie, Brucie, Brucie" she would call as she skipped to meet him, and she would chatter away to him.

One evening the family was gathered in the living room. Karen was sitting on the floor intent on her coloring when Bruce asked her:

"Karen, do you remember before you were born?"

"Yes."

"What was it like?"

"It was red and there was lots of water."

"Is that why you like to swim so much?"

"Yes."

"Do you remember what it was like before you were in your Mama's tummy?"

"Yes."

"What was it like?"

"I don't talk about that."

And she went back to coloring.

NANCY HOLT

Janet's Story

I KNEW A CHILD whose mother had two stillborn children before this third child was born healthy. The mother would often go to the cemetery where the two infants were buried, taking her child along. One day, the child said to her, "Why do you take me there? They are me and I am here."

JANET MCGAVIN

Renate

A FOUR YEAR OLD said to his aunt: "Do you know, Auntie, I should have actually come to you. You see, it was like this. I was with a lot of other people a long way away from earth, in heaven. And suddenly an old man came and called out: 'Go, Renate, you have to go down now!' And so it started up. I was whirled around the earth. That went in all directions so incredibly fast. And then I passed by your window, but I could not get in. So I flew further, and Mummy's window was open, and I could get in there. And so I came to Mummy, but actually I should have come to you!"

REPORTED BY O.J. HARTMAN

Mother

MY MOTHER WAS BORN IN 1906 and told me that her earliest memory was of being in a blank void. There were other 'beings' with her and they were looking down a tunnel at a woman lying in a bed. The 'beings' told my mother that she could choose this life if she wished, but the end of her 'story' was not written and she would have to take a chance on how it would end. My mother felt that she could not disappoint this woman who had had other disappointments, and said she chose life. With that she felt as though she were sliding, and there was a bright light, and she was born!

My grandmother had had a series of miscarriages after the birth of her first child and my mother was very much wanted.

JANET PARSONS

Sibling Awareness

Jessica

OUR NOT-YET-FOUR YEAR OLD, JESSICA, listened quietly as her father and I discussed names for the coming baby—girls' names and boys' names.

Finally she said, a little impatiently, "Mommy, her name is Alia. She's a girl."

And she was. And we named her Alia.

ROBIN OLSON

Emma & Alexandra

I HAD MY CHILDREN LATER IN LIFE (second marriage and two step children already), and so we only planned on having one.

When my first daughter, Emma, was five, we were doing the bed-time routine (story, prayer, etc.) when she said to me: "Mummy, last night when I was in heaven I was talking to grandpa, and he said my sister was there and waiting to be born-ed, so when will she?" I was rather stunned, and did the usual, "Well, when she's ready" reply…and went to speak to my husband! Ok, so let's see, we said…and …around nine months later there she was!

And therein lies another story:

This second daughter was nearly two weeks overdue. My mother, who came over for a month for the birth from Cape

93

Town in South Africa, where she lives, only had two weeks left of her trip, and was getting anxious. We had already chosen her name (of course we knew it was going to be a girl from Emma's chats with her grandpa in heaven), which was a combination of family names—Ami-Beth. My mother, a wise kindergarten teacher and eurythmist said: "Well, maybe she doesn't like that name. Anyone who is this strong—to decide on her birth date in such a way—needs a stronger name." That night, a new name came to me—and a few hours later, Alexandra Sophia finally joined her sister who had been waiting for her for such a long time!

And she really is an Alexandra! She has just turned eighteen—a strong, purposeful, and wise child!

And so, we are blessed with two beautiful daughters.

JANNI NICOL

A new baby boy

MY YOUNGEST CHILD was due; I was busy sewing some last things for the baby. My five old and six year old were playing, as so often, in the adjacent room with their little friend. Suddenly, one of them said, "Look! Above the hill is the baby. It's coming!" Another answered, "I see it. It's coming."

Shortly after, labor began, and approximately two hours later a healthy boy was born at home.

AILEEN NIESSEN

Sibling Rivalry

MY SIX-YEAR-OLD DAUGHTER and four-year-old adopted son woke up one morning very grumpy. They argued as they got dressed and bickered over breakfast. I decided as it was a nice day and they were up early we would walk to school in hopes of losing the "grumps" on the way. But to no avail. They found every reason to grumble all the way to school. Normally they got on very well and to be walking to school with them was quite delightful, but not on that day.

Eventually we arrived at kindergarten. My daughter went into her group and my son into his. I sighed a huge sigh of relief and went home.

When I returned to collect them both for their lunch I was really fed up to hear that the bickering had not abated. We got to the end of the corridor to the outside door whereupon my daughter made some triumphant statement which she obviously thought would outdo anything her brother could think of and then she stomped off ahead of us. Her brother just stood there watching her go and said "I was *so* glad when she got borned and left me in peace in heaven."

I have loved this story ever since it happened, particularly because of the adoption involved and the fact they certainly believed they were together before they were born.

JANET KLAAR

Maebelle

I WAS PLANNING my third home birth. When I was eight weeks pregnant, I told my four-year-old daughter there was a baby on the way. Maebelle immediately announced to her pre-kindergarten teacher that I had two babies in my tummy, a girl and a boy—one for her and one for her brother. I tried the entire pregnancy to convince her there was probably only one so she wouldn't be disappointed but she held to her story.

At thirty-six weeks, there was reason for possible concern so I had an ultrasound and it was confirmed then, much to my husband's and my surprise, that I was indeed carrying two babies, a girl and a boy. "I told you, Mom," Maebelle said loudly.

I carried the babies for two more nights and Maebelle would ask me, "Where is the boy? Where is the girl?" I would point to the side they were on and she would whisper good night to them.

She was there for the birth and watched me deliver them one by one. I've never seen a four year old so happy and proud of herself.

ALISA M. HACKL-WEISS

Noah

NOT VERY LONG AFTER my son's second birthday, I was standing in the bathroom brushing my teeth when suddenly he came running up from behind and head butted me in my tush as hard as he could. Having gotten my complete attention, he looked up at me and demanded, "Where is my sister baby?" as if a sister baby was something that had been promised to him for a very long time and he was tired of waiting patiently for the promise to be kept. My husband and I had no plans for a second child at the time, but within two months I was pregnant with our daughter.

When my son was six and my daughter was three, I had the most wonderful dream in which I was told that I would have a third child. His name would be Noah. Neither my husband nor I particularly wanted a third child, but in the dream there was this wonderful sense that it would all be okay and that I was not to worry about getting pregnant, that it would just happen when the time was right.

Less than a year later, my father-in-law moved in with us. He had been a diabetic for nearly 60 years, had had a stroke eight years earlier, and was generally not in the greatest of health. After about a year and a half, he was diagnosed with a fast moving, very invasive form of thyroid cancer. The radiation and chemo-therapies were hard on his already compromised health. He needed twenty-four-hour care, and the bulk of that care fell to my husband and me. I was exhausted all the time and had completely forgotten the dream about Noah.

One day while driving home from church I had the feeling that there was another being or beings in the car with me — not that they were physically present in a material sense, but that there was an opening into the spirit world through which they were reaching. Noah had come to tell me that he loved me, loved what I was doing in the world. He would not be coming after all because it would be too much for me. There was this sense that he was so proud of me and loved me so much, that he would miss me terribly. It was like reaching hands across the widening gap of water as someone you love departs on a boat. There was also the sense that he was not alone, but with a whole host of loving beings who were there to witness and support both of us as we said goodbye to our relationship before it ever had the chance to start in the physical world. I remember being so relieved and so sad at the same time. The experience was so real that I have this odd sense of both grieving for a child that I lost and loving a most amazing child that I never had in the physical world.

MARY BETH MUELLER

Other Lives

Tom

It was a glorious day, near midday, in Durban, South Africa, back in 1971. Our two young sons, ages three and four, were playing happily in the garden; I was hanging the washing on the line to dry in the kind of sun that only Africa can provide. Suddenly there was a tug on my blouse. Tom, our four year old, was standing beside me looking earnest, apologetic, and a little rushed, having briefly broken away from his game with Simon. "Mommy, I don't want you to be sad," he said, "but you're not my first mommy. I have had many mommies before you." That said, he dashed back to his game with Simon and never referred to the matter again.

ROBIN LAWTON

Shoes

My two-and-a-half-year-old son was sitting on the bed with his little legs stuck straight out in front of him, watching quietly as I tied his shoes, when he said thoughtfully, "I used to be able to tie my own shoes."

JO ANN JEFFRIES

Laurens

ONE SATURDAY MORNING, the family was relaxing around the table having just finished breakfast. My son and daughter-in-law were sitting opposite my husband and me. My four-year-old grandson, Laurens, was sitting on my lap, still nibbling on some toast, when out of the blue he said, quite matter-of-factly:

"That's not my mother."

"Who is she?" my husband asked.

"My mother's dead."

"When did she die?"

"1918."

"Your mother died in 1918?"

"Yes, she died of the flu."

"Did anyone else die?"

"No."

"What was your mother's name?"

"Mama."

"Where did you live?"

"Orange County."

"What was your name?"

"Mark."

"What was the rest of your name?"

"Mark James."

He was quiet awhile. Then he said:

"I have a now Mama."

NANCY HOLT

Eve

EVE WAS FOUR AND A HALF when she heard that Uncle Fred had died.

When I told Eve of Uncle Fred's death she said:

"When will God make Uncle Fred another time? If He doesn't make him another time, I'll cry."

HELEN EVANS
From a letter to her mother, February 12, 1939

Long lost child

A YOUNG DIVORCED MOTHER was living in a new relationship and was expecting a child. She had a miscarriage and lost the child. Shortly after, she had to flee from the father of her first two children, which forced the new relationship to come to an end.

She trained as a dyslexia consultant and years went by. She had two very dear friends who had three children. They asked if she would work with their youngest, who was dyslexic. The mother and the child picked her up at the train station. When she stepped out of the train, the child, seeing her for the first time, walked over to her, took her hand, and said, "You are my mother." Indeed, her birthday was approximately nine months after the miscarriage.

AILEEN NIESSEN

Glimpses
across
the
Threshold

True Love

MOSES MENDELSSOHN, grandfather of the well-known German composer, was far from being handsome. Along with a rather short stature, he had a grotesque hunchback.

One day he visited a merchant in Hamburg who had a lovely daughter named Frumtje. Moses fell hopelessly in love with her. But Frumtje was repulsed by his misshapen appearance.

When it came time for him to leave, Moses gathered his courage and climbed the stairs to her room to take one last opportunity to speak with her. She was a vision of heavenly beauty, but caused him deep sadness by her refusal to look at him. After several attempts at conversation, Moses shyly asked, "Do you believe marriages are made in heaven?"

"Yes," she answered, still looking at the floor. "And do you?"

"Yes, I do," he replied. "You see, in heaven at the birth of each boy, the Lord announces which girl he will marry. When I was born, my future bride was pointed out to me. Then the Lord added, 'But your wife will be humpbacked.'

"Right then and there I called out, 'Oh Lord, a humpbacked woman would be a tragedy. Please, Lord, give me the hump and let her be beautiful."

Then Frumtje looked up into his eyes and was stirred by some deep memory. She reached out and gave Mendelssohn her hand and later became his devoted wife.

BARRY AND JOYCE VISSELL

Stories of the Unborn Soul

I WAS BORN IN 1965 and man wasn't able to view earth as I saw it, until astronauts went to the moon. As a child, when I first saw the photos of the earth taken from space, it was exactly as I remembered it. I can also remember that, while still in the spiritual, the physical world seemed as unreal as the spiritual does from the physical perspective.

MICHAEL MAGUIRE
Quoted in Stories of the Unborn Soul *by Elisabeth Hallet*

MY MOTHER MADE SUCH A BIG DEAL of the first men walking on the moon, she told me to watch and exclaimed, "Oh, that's what earth looks like from outer space!" I thought she was off her rocker. Hadn't she seen what earth looked like from outer space before? Ah well, that was before I realized I was the weird one!

KATHY
Quoted in Stories of the Unborn Soul *by Elisabeth Hallett*

Memories from Three Women

"I hovered around my mother."

"I felt as though my region of movement was restricted to a certain radius around my mother which grew smaller as the day of birth approached."

"I was outside the fetus. I watched in amazement at this form developing, knowing it would become mine, protecting it with my own energy as well as my mothers."

HELEN WAMBACH
from Life Before Life

The Third Group of People

HE SAID THAT THREE GROUPS of people lived in every village.

First were those you could see—walking around, eating, sleeping, and working.

Second were the ancestors, whom Grandma Yaisa had now joined.

"And the third people—who are they?" asked Kunta.

"The third people," said Omoro, "are those waiting to be born."

ALEX HALEY
1921 – 1992
from Roots

The New One

Annabel had just been born. Sunlight and Breeze had been to visit and now Starling and his Fledgling were perched on the side of the cradle.

"Good girl!" croaked the Starling approvingly. He cocked his head on one side and gazed at her with his round bright eye. "I hope," he remarked politely, "you are not too tired after your journey."

Annabel shook her head.

"Where has she come from—out of an egg?" cheeped the Fledgling suddenly.

"Huh-huh!" scoffed Mary Poppins. "Do you think she's a sparrer?"

The Starling gave her a pained and haughty look.

"Well, what is she then? And where did she come from?" cried the Fledgling shrilly, flapping his short wings and staring down at the cradle.

"You tell him, Annabel!" the Starling croaked.

Annabel moved her hands inside the blanket.

"I am earth and air and fire and water," she said softly. "I come from the Dark where all things have their beginning."

"Ah, such dark!" said the Starling softly, bending his head to his breast.

"It was dark in the egg, too," the Fledging cheeped.

"I come from the sea and its tides," Annabel went on. "I come from the sky and its stars. I come from the sun and its brightness—"

"Ah, so bright!" said the Starling, nodding.

"And I come from the forests of earth."

As if in a dream, Mary Poppins rocked the cradle—to-and-fro, to-and-fro with a steady swinging movement.

"Yes?" whispered the Fledgling.

"Slowly I moved at first," said Annabel, "always sleeping and dreaming. I remembered all that I had been and I thought of all I shall be. And when I had dreamed my dream I awoke and came swiftly."

She paused for a moment, her blue eyes full of memories.

"And then?" prompted the Fledgling.

"I heard the stars singing as I came and I felt warm wings about me. I passed the beasts of the jungle and came through the dark, deep waters. It was a long journey."

Annabel was silent.

The Fledgling stared at her with his bright inquisitive eyes.

Mary Poppins' hand lay quietly on the side of the cradle. She had stopped rocking.

"A long journey indeed!" said the Starling softly, lifting his head from his breast. "And, ah, so soon forgotten!"

Annabel stirred under the quilt.

"No!" she said confidently. "I'll never forget."

"Stuff and Nonsense, Beaks and Claws, of course you will! By the time the week's out you won't remember a word of it— what you are or where you came from!"

Inside her flannel petticoat Annabel was kicking furiously.

"I will! I will! How could I forget?"

"Because they all do!" jeered the Starling harshly. "Every silly human except—" he nodded his head at Mary Poppins— "her! She's Different, she's the Oddity, she's the Misfit—"

"I don't believe you! I won't believe you!" cried Annabel wildly.

P.L. TRAVERS
1899 – 1966
from Mary Poppins Comes Back

The Angel of Conception

AMONG THE ANGELS there is one who serves as the midwife of souls. This is Lailah, the angel of conception. When the time has come for conception, Lailah seeks out a certain soul hidden in the Garden of Eden and commands it to enter the seed. The soul is always reluctant, for it still remembers the pain of being born, and it prefers to remain pure. But Lailah compels the soul to obey, and that is how new life comes into being.

While the infant grows in the womb, Lailah watches over it, reading the unborn child the history of its soul. All the while a light shines upon the head of the child, by which it sees from one end of the world to the other. And Lailah shows the child the rewards of the Garden of Eden, as well as the punishments of Gehenna. But when the time has come to be born, the angel extinguishes the light and brings forth the child into the world, and as it is brought forth, it cries. Then Lailah lightly strikes the newborn above the lip, causing it to forget all it has learned. And that is the origin of this mark, which everyone bears.

Indeed, Lailah is a guardian angel who watches over us all of our days. And when the time has come to take leave of this world, it is Lailah who leads us to the World to Come.

JEWISH RABBINIC TALE, BABYLON: 5TH C.
from Gabriel's Palace: Jewish Mystical Tales *by Howard Schwartz*

Birthdays are cause for delightful celebrations in Waldorf School kindergartens around the world. Teachers are free to elaborate the story to suit each child and the family's situation. Following are two examples.

Kathleen's Nursery Birthday Story

Once upon a time, up in the heavens, there dwelled a shining star. The star looked down to the earth and saw a wondrous place. The star said to his angel, "I would like to go there." The little star looked far and wide over the whole earth, until he found a woman with love in her heart and a twinkle in her eye. The star said, "I want her to be my mother." The star found a man loving and kind and the star told his angel, "I want him to be my father."

And so the angel accompanied the star on his journey from the heavens, over the Rainbow Bridge down to the earth and into the waiting arms of his parents who named him: Matthew.

Ameli's Kindergarten Birthday Story

ONCE UPON A TIME there lived a mother and a father and they longed to have a child. At that time a little angel looked down from the heavens onto the earth and thought, "Oh, how beautiful the earth is with its rivers and seas, the trees and flowers, the animals, the people working together to make the earth a good place to live." The little angel began to long to be on the beautiful earth. The longing grew and one day she went to her guardian angel and asked, "Please may I go and live on the earth and play and work?" The guardian angel answered, "Yes, but first you must make yourself a garment for your journey. Come with me in the morning and I will show you what you must do."

The next day the little angel got up early and the guardian angel took the little angel to the see the Sun. "Let us build a palace for the Sun," instructed the guardian angel. All day the little angel worked and by nightfall they had built a beautiful palace for the Sun. The Sun thanked the little angel and gave her a golden ray of sunlight. The little angel kept the precious gift close to her heart.

The next day they journeyed to the Moon and in turn built a fine palace for the Moon. And the Moon also gave the little angel a gift. It was a silver ray of moonlight. The little angel kept it close to her heart.

On the third day the task was to build a palace for the Stars. When the palace was finished each star in turn gave the little angel a shining ray of starlight.

Now the little angel was ready to make a garment for herself. The little angel wove and wove and when the garment was made the little angel fell into a deep sleep.

Meanwhile on the earth a loving Father and Mother began to prepare for a child to be born. And when the time was right the Guardian Angel awoke the little angel, and together they went to the Rainbow Bridge where they said goodbye to one another. That day a new baby was born on the earth. And the Mother and Father received their child with great joy.

AUTHOR UNKNOWN

A Childhood Memory

YOUNG CHILDREN DO NOT NEED to ask where they have come from or why they are here, for they bring the answers to these questions with them. This intuitive knowledge is often lost, at least from consciousness, as adulthood closes round the child. One small memory is all I can recall of those golden years, now over forty-five years distant. It has not been a passive memory in any sense, but rather one that I realize in hindsight, has played an active role in making me the person that I am.

As a little girl, long after I was supposed to be asleep at night, I would creep out of my bed and stand by the open door that led from my bedroom out into the garden. From this threshold I would gaze up at the night sky and talk and sing to the stars. In such moments I remembered a conversation I had with God before I came down to earth:

    Ann was called before God and He asked her,

    "Ann, do you love Me?"

    Ann replied,

    "Yes, God. I do."

    God asked the question again,

    "Ann, do you love Me?"

    Ann was concerned because she thought God knew that she loved him so she answered,

    "But, God, You know that I love You!"

    A third time God asked the question,

    "Ann, do you love Me?"

    Ann could only reply,

    "Lord, what must I do to show You that I love You?"

    God replied,

    "I am going to send you far away from Me. I want you to find your way back. Furthermore, I am going to take away from you all memory of Me. Through your love for Me, seek your way back."

    And with that God sent Ann to earth.

ANN LANG
1943 – 2006

Sachi

SOON AFTER HER BROTHER WAS BORN, little Sachi began to ask her parents to leave her alone with the new baby. They worried that like most four year olds, she might feel jealous and want to hit or shake him, so they said no. But she showed no signs of jealousy. She treated the baby with kindness, and her pleas to be left alone with him became more urgent. They decided to allow it.

Elated, she went into the baby's room and shut the door, but it opened a crack—enough for her curious parents to peek in and listen. They saw little Sachi walk quietly up to her baby brother, put her face close to his and say quietly, "Baby, tell me what God feels like. I'm starting to forget."

DAN MILLMAN

Words of Wisdom from Janet

JANET McGAVIN (1915-1994), who attended many births as a nurse midwife, used to say,

"When we are born, we weep and all around us rejoice, and when we die, we rejoice and all around us weep."

SUSAN HOWARD

Remembering My Birth

I HAVE STRONG MEMORIES of the time prior to my birth. I remember having infinite possibilities of this life communicated to me and of my having to agree to accept this life. Time really does not define how long this lasted.

During my early childhood, it seemed to me quite natural that everyone remembered their birth. Yet, as I began to verbalize this knowledge, I found that mine is an unusual memory. As a young child, I remember asking my mother on many occasions if she remembered the day I got my sight. This request was frequently met with a puzzled look. I would try to explain that I wasn't totally blind, but that my perception of light was very dim or shaded.

The actual birth was cold and antiseptic. The change in my surroundings was startling. I went from a subdued existence into literally being pulled into a brightness that was extremely disquieting. (As a child I would ask my mom if "they" pulled or squeezed my head to give me sight. Later, I found out that mine was a cesarean birth). The light was intense and not from a natural source—not that I knew that then. Simply, the light was not a source of heat. I sensed being rubbed only around my face which led me to believe in my early years that this rubbing brought about my eyesight.

I also remember that the walls of the hospital were green.

TIA HALL

Nascuntur Poetae . . .†

We are gazing into some strange incomprehensible painting of Piero di Cosimo; a world of pale blues and greens; of abrupt peaks in agate and of walled cities; of flying red stags with hounds at their throats; and of lions in tears beside their crowns. On the roads are seen traveling companies, in no haste and often lost in contemplation of the sky. A boy sits on a rock in the foreground. He is listening to the words of a woman dressed in a chlamys that takes on the color of the objects about her.

THE WOMAN IN THE CHLAMYS: In a far valley, boy, sit those who in their lifetime have possessed some special gift of eye or ear or finger. There they sit apart, choosing their successors. And when on the winds toward birth the souls of those about to live are borne past them, they choose the brighter spirits that cry along that wind. And you were chosen.

THE BOY: For what gift, lady, did the choice fall? Am I to mould in clay, or paint? Shall I sing or mime, lady? What choice fell on me and from what master?

THE WOMAN IN THE CHLAMYS: It is enough to know that you were chosen.

THE BOY: What further remains to be done? You have poured on my eyes and ears and mouth the divine ointment; you have laid on my tongue the burning ember. Why do we delay?

---

† Nascuntur poetae, fiunt oratores. (Cicero)
 'Poets are born, orators are made.'

THE WOMAN IN THE CHLAMYS: Be not so eager for life. Too soon you will be shaken by breath; too soon and too long you will be tossed in the tumult of the senses.

THE BOY: I am not afraid of life. I will astonish it. Why are we delaying?

THE WOMAN IN THE CHLAMYS: My sister is coming now. Listen to her. [*The woman in the chlamys withdraws and gives place to her sister, whose feet stir not the shells upon the path. She wears a robe of deep and noble red and bears in her hands a long golden chain hung about with pendants. Her face is fixed in concentration and compassion, like the face of one taking part in a sacrifice of great moment.*]

THE BOY: All is ready. What do you come to do?

THE WOMAN IN DEEP RED: My sister has given you the gifts of pride and of joy. But those are not all.

THE BOY: What gifts remain? I have been chosen. I am ready.

THE WOMAN IN DEEP RED: Those gifts are vain without these. He who carries much gold stumbles. I bring the dark and necessary gifts. This golden chain…

THE BOY: [*With mounting fear*] Your face is shadowed. Draw back, take back all the gifts, if I must accept these also.

THE WOMAN IN DEEP RED: Too late. Too late. You had no choice in this. You must bow your head.

THE BOY: I am trembling. My knees are hot with my tears.

THE WOMAN IN DEEP RED: Since only tears can give sight to the eyes. [*She drops the chain about his neck.*]

THE BOY: Then am I permitted to know the meaning of these pendants?

THE WOMAN IN DEEP RED: This is a tongue of fire. It feeds upon the brain. It is a madness that in a better country has a better name.

THE BOY: These are mysteries. Give them no names.

THE WOMAN IN DEEP RED: This is a leaf of laurel from a tree not often plucked. You shall know pride and the shining of the eyes—of that I do not speak now.

THE BOY: And this, lady?

THE WOMAN IN DEEP RED: That is a staff and signifies the journey that awaits you your life long; for you are homeless.

THE BOY: And this…this is of crystal….

THE WOMAN IN DEEP RED: That is yours alone, and you shall smart for it. It is wonderful and terrible. Others shall know a certain peace and shall live well enough in the limits of the life they know; but you shall be forever hindered. For you there shall be ever beyond the present a lost meaning and a more meaningful love.

THE BOY: Take back the chain. Take back your gifts. Take back life. For at its end what can there be that is worth such pain?

THE WOMAN IN DEEP RED: [*Slowly drawing back into the shadow of the wood.*] Farewell, child of the muses, playfellow in the bird-haunted groves. The life of man awaits you, the light laughter and the misery in the same day, in the selfsame hour the trivial and the divine. You are to give it a voice. Among the bewildered and the stammering thousands you are to give it a voice and to mark its meaning. Farewell, child of the muses, playfellow in the bird-haunted.... [THE WOMAN IN THE CHLAMYS *returns.*]

THE WOMAN IN THE CHLAMYS: You must go now. Listen to that wind. It is the great fan of time that whirls on the soul for a season.

THE BOY: Stay a moment. I am not yet brave.

[*She leads him into a grotto and the young soul and his chain are lost in the profound shade.*]

THORNTON WILDER
1897-1975

The Cherokee people believe they came from the stars—the seven-pointed star—and that is why their council hut has seven sides.

CHEROKEE LORE

Creation Myth of The Cherokee Indian
An Adaption for Performance

This is what the old folks told me they had heard when they were young:
  [♪ *Music – ethereal, timeless*]
    [*Gradual appearance of Sky People*]

Sky – y – y – y
Sky people
    people
       people of the sky
        y – y – y
High above in Galunlati

  [♪ *Ethereal, timeless, changing to varied
  to suggest different animals*]

Panther and beaver
Spider – spinner – weaver
Weaver – spinner – spider
Beetle and turtle
These sky people
Rabbit and eagle
   and bear

All were there
With Selu
Mother of the corn, Selu
And Kanati the Hunter
Kanati with his bow
   Long ago, long ago

[♪ *Timeless quality*]

Many were the sky people
  long ago, long ago
    coming and going
      in Galunlati
        going and coming
High above in Galunlati
  High above in the highest place
    In the seventh height
      Beyond the vault of the sky
Sky people star people
  People of the seven-pointed star
    Far above in the seventh height
      Galunlati was their home
        Om, om

[♪ *Discord, anxiety*]

Now it grew crowded
  'owded, ow, ow
In the sky y – y – y
Sky people too many
  oo, oo, oo
Fearful of falling
        falling
          falling

Down
   down
      down
         drawn down

[♪ *Falling*]

What was below – ow – ow – ow?
Water, water
All was water
And below the water?
   Who knows?
      Who knows?
      Who knows?

'I will go
    I will go
        I will go'

Water beetle, beaver's grandchild
   Go and see, what's below
      So we'll know

Beetle darted
Beetle swam
   over water
East he swam
   and West
North he swam
   and South
No place found
   for flipper or foot

Beetle dived
deep under
down he went
and then
mud he found
and when
up he brought it
Oh
watch it grow
in all directions

[♪ *Primal chaos – gradual form – mud growing*]

Sky people are amazed
Sky people are astonished

Quickly spider
Spin your threads
Twist a rope
to tie the earth
    North and South
    East and West
Tie the earth to Galunlati

[♪ *Weaving*]

Sky people see that it is done
See the earth is set below
Smooth and glistening there it lies
Slowly dries

Earth are you ready?
Earth are you steady?
    Rock ready for standing?

Chickadee flew to see
  East he flew
    and West
  North he flew
    and South
No place could he find to rest

[♪ *Time passes in Galunlati*]

Earth are you ready?
Earth are you steady?
  Held fast and firm
  For foot fall?

Redbird flew to see
  East he flew
    and West
  North he flew
    and South
No place could he find to rest
  I fly, I fly
  No place is dry

[♪ *Time passes in Galunlati*]

Surely now the time must be
Eagle, Eagle fly and see

Eagle flew
And strongly swept
High above the earth
Then low he swooped
And mountains leapt
Where he struck the earth

Country of the Cherokee
Filled with mountains high you see

[♪ *Eagle flight*]

Soon earth is dry
Sky folk come to live on land
But all is dark
Set the sun to go above
East to West just overhead
Crawfish shell is scorched bright red!
Set the sun one handbreadth higher
Still too hot
So higher still
Till seven handbreadths high
It stands today just right

[♪ *Sun dance, fading into gathering earth
and flowing water* ♪]

Now Earth
has gathered herself
Grasses grow and pines
Cedars, sourwood too
In the valley flows the river
Sacred ceremonial water
For the Cherokee
He 'Long Person' river
Head in mountain
Foot in valley
Healing water for people
Water of life for Cherokee

[♪ *Water music – changing*]

And to this day
there is still
coming and going
going and coming
between Galunlati and Earth
between Earth and Galunlati

[♪ *Coming and going*]

This is what the old folks told me they had heard when they were young.

EVE OLIVE
January, 1981
Adapted from The Cherokee Creation Myth
and other Cherokee stories

NOTE: The presently accepted version of the Cherokee Creation Myth speaks of the Buzzard rather than the Eagle. However, some earlier versions of the myth, which inspired this work, featured the Eagle as co-creator of the earth. For this story, the author has chosen the Eagle.

*Speaking
of
Angels*

The Angel that presided o'er my birth
Said, "Little creature, form'd of joy and mirth,
Go, love without the help of any thing on earth."

→ WILLIAM BLAKE
1757-1827

Why do we keep them waiting? — Angels are
More affable than earthly folk, by far!

→ PERCY MACKAYE
1875 – 1956

The Angel

An angel was crossing the pale vault of night,
    and his song was as soft as his flight,
and the moon and the stars and the clouds in a throng
    stood enthralled by this holy song.

He sang of the bliss of the innocent shades
    in the depths of celestial glades;
he sang of the Sovereign Being, and free
    of guile was his eulogy.

He carried a soul in his arms, a young life
    to the world of sorrow and strife,
and the young soul retained the throb of that song
    —without words, but vivid and strong.

And tied to this planet long did it pine
    full of yearnings dimly divine,
and our dull little ditties could never replace
    songs belonging to infinite space.

➔ MIKHAIL LERMONTOV
1814 – 1841
Translated from the Russian
by Vladimir Nabokov

Annunciation

The messenger of God, in swirling mantle, came,
  O so gently to my place of slumber
And, bending low to me, he said the words:
  Be patient still for just a little longer,
  the boy is now already on his way!–

And like the sound of wind in velvet curtains,
  in one quick flash, the holding of a breath,
The silence broke, and lo! I heard it clearly,
  your footsteps, child,
  your footsteps coming, coming to me,
  from distant hills, from far away.

→ INA SEIDEL
1885 – 1974
Translated from the German
by Pauline Wehrle

Angel of the Twilight

I leave you
Angel of the twilight
leave me not

Earth beckons
Follow!
I see you not

Be near me in the darkness of earth light
Meet me in the light of heaven's night

Angel of the twilight
leave me not

➔ EVE OLIVE
1934 –
from Words for a Child

Angel and Man

Written in January, 1898, at the age of 23, and found after his death in a notebook.

IN THE HEART OF HUMANKIND—woman as well as her lover—dwell two, angel and man. Both are good. Angel is serene, because he is independent of the material world; man is perplexed, because he is dependent. In the case of a true man or woman, man and angel love each other dearly, and each learns from the other.

But man is the more helpless, and in all his woes, rests in the arms of angel, for the arms of angel are eternal. Angel comes from a place ignorant of space and time called heaven, and he comes to man who dwells in the land of time and space called earth in order that he may reveal himself–for heaven without earth is barren.

Angel, then, needs man, in order to become perfect through his revelation in the flesh–which revelation is called beauty.

Man needs angel in order to become perfect through his resurrection from the flesh–which resurrection is called virtue. And the love of man for angel is called faith: and the love of angel for man–inspiration, and that realm which is the meeting ground of both–that realm is called imagination, or the country of mystery, the borderland of truth where neither man nor angel, but only God, yet has trod.

In thinking of ourselves, therefore, we must remember that we are the mysterious abiding-place of man and angel, and we must not think that the laws and customs which govern man apply necessarily to angel, or vice versa. But we must allow each to help the other to the full extent of the powers granted to each by his peculiar world.

Angel must not long to fly away back to heaven, without man, nor man hunger to eat his meal of earth unshared by angel.

→ PERCY MACKAYE
1875 – 1956

from The Soul of Man

Between morning and evening the angel carries the soul around, and shows her where she will live and where she will die, and the place where she will be buried, and she takes her through the whole world, and points out the just and the sinners and all things. In the evening, she replaces her in the womb of the mother and there she remains for nine months.

➤ JEWISH LEGEND
retold by LOUIS GINZBERG
1873 – 1953

O My Angel

O my Angel, spread your wings
And bear me to the source of things—

Far into the world of light
Hidden in the heart of night.

O my Angel, let me sleep—
Bathe me in the star-bright deep.

Bathe my being bright and clean—
Heal me in the vast unseen.

➜ ARVIA MACKAYE EGE
1902 – 1989

Meditations
and
Prayers

For Expectant Mothers

Light and Warmth

Light and warmth
Of the divine spirit world
Envelope me.

Before the Birth

And the child's soul
Be given to me
According to your will
Out of the worlds of spirit.

After the Birth

And the child's soul
Be guided by me
According to your will
Into the world of spirit.

→ RUDOLF STEINER
1861 – 1925

Meditation for Mothers

Into my will
Let there pour strength,
Into my feeling
Let there flow warmth,
Into my thinking
Let there shine light,
That I may nurture this child
With enlightened purpose,
Caring with heart's love
And bringing wisdom
Into all things.

→ JOAN SALTER
1912 – 2004

Prayer for Small Children
Spoken by an Adult

Into you stream light that can grip you
I accompany its rays with the warmth of my love.
I think with the best joyous thoughts of my thinking
    On the stirrings of your heart:
    They shall strengthen you,
    They shall support you,
    They shall clarify you.
I should like to gather into your life-steps
    My joyous thoughts,
That they bind themselves to your will for life;
And it find itself in strength
In all the world
Ever more through itself.

↛ RUDOLF STEINER
1861 – 1925
Translated from the German
by Arvia MacKaye Ege

A Child's Evening Prayer

From my head to my feet
I'm the picture of God.
From my heart into my hands
I feel God's living breath.
When I speak with my mouth
I follow God's own will.
When I gaze on God
In the whole world-all,
In father and mother,
In all dear people,
In beast and flower,
In tree and stone,
No fear can come near,
Only love
For all that's around me here.

→ RUDOLF STEINER
1861 – 1925
Translated from the German
by Arvia MacKaye Ege

Postlude

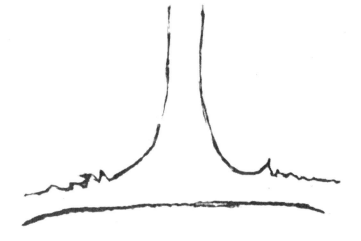

Don't Run Go Slowly

Don't run, go slowly,
It is only to yourself that you have to go!

Go slowly, don't run,
For the child of yourself, just born
And eternal
Cannot follow you.

✈ JUAN RAMÓN JIMÉNEZ
1881-1958
Translated from the Spanish
by H.R. Hays

Coda

Coda

Why do we tend to focus on the possibility of a life after death and generally fail to consider the possibility of a life before birth? Are we in fact all 'prodigal sons' in this life, setting off with our gifts, and returning one day to our Father's house? Is our birth into this world perhaps the greatest mystery of all?

THIS COLLECTION OF POEMS AND STORIES MIGHT HAVE ended here—a gift to delight and inspire different people in different ways. Yet to see before us such a rich collection of works spread across cultures, languages, and epochs suggests that these varied perceptions—these inspired glimpses from the threshold of birth—point to a story of our lives that makes sense in a more comprehensive way. A quiet thought beckons, that they hold seeds of truth, clues to the profound questions of existence. Who are we? Why are we here? What is this life all about? Do we come into this world consciously and with intention? Langston Hughes assuredly felt that he did: "Like stroke / Of lightning / In the night / Some mark / To make / Some word / To tell." Perhaps, as he suggests, we come from a realm of light, of mystery: "Oh, fields of wonder / Out of which / Stars are born." Or as Wordsworth says, "trailing clouds of glory do we come / From God, who is our home."

Even more perplexing, do we just happen to be born to particular parents, or do we seek them out, as Elizabeth Spires describes in her poem 'Worldling'? Nelly Sachs suggests in 'Chorus of the Unborn' that we actually help to bring our parents together. If each of our mothers had married someone else, would you still be you, would I still be me? If we'd had different fathers would you—as you know yourself—and I— as I know myself—simply not have existed? A sobering thought. The weight of scientific evidence insists that our existence is the result of a genetic combination of DNA from our parents, yet some still small voice continually whispers that our true being is something that transcends the body we find ourselves living in. In spite of all of these challenging questions, it seems clear that somehow in each of us is an awareness that: I am.

In their uncollected state, scattered as so many leaves around the globe, these poems and stories perhaps do little more than suggest some interesting ideas. Yet brought together to live side by side on the page, a pattern appears and suggests a deeper mystery. The poems pulse with the sense that we are not created as souls at the moment of conception or of first breath, but are in fact spirit/soul beings who enjoyed a life in a spiritual realm before this life on earth. Ever and again the poets suggest that we are drawn to this physical life, that we have some purpose in mind. Do we choose to come to particular parents because they can give us what we need for our further development on earth? Do we come when we do because we need to be here at a certain time in history? Think of a Churchill, a Gandhi, a Martin Luther King, Jr., a Mandela.

Do we take an interest in, and perhaps even participate in, the development of our bodies in the womb? The research of Helen Wambach, Ph.D., suggests that we do, and from across the centuries Rumi tells us, "We made / the body, / cell by cell / we made it." A powerful picture arises in which we participate with interest and together with the great creative powers of the universe in bringing that little body into being— the body we will 'wear' in this life. As Mary Oliver says, "The spirit / likes to dress up like this: / ten fingers, / ten toes, / shoulders, and all the rest."

And what about angels—and perhaps even higher spiritual beings who were recognized and celebrated in former times? Do they exist, and if so, are they also involved in this mysterious process of birth? In his poem 'The Angel,' Lermontov pictures the angel bringing a soul to earth. Do these beings sometimes announce our coming, as in Ina Seidel's poem 'Annunciation'? Perhaps they remain with us throughout life, helping us to unfold our destiny, as Alfred Baur pictures in 'A Different Moon': "The unborn child— / so long as it is growing in the mother's womb / its angel tells the story of its life, / and writes it into the body's becoming." Do we come with a destiny—with certain challenges we will have to face and certain gifts we need to share? Baur speaks of the "duty-bound calling" of the angel to help us with this destiny.

Meditating on these pictures suggests that the whole

process of pregnancy, and indeed childhood, is a time when the soul is transitioning from consciousness in another realm to consciousness on the earth: "falling asleep / to the home I have known / I awake / here on the earth" (Olive). It is worth noting that most of the stories in the section, "The Things Children Say," come from children younger than five. There are just two examples of a significant memory from a seven year old and a nine year old. The little stories concerning sibling awareness—who is coming next—suggest 'contracts' made before birth, agreements to be together in this life.

Then there are those children who remember other lives. Is it possible that only some of us have had previous lives on earth, or is this perhaps a shared human experience, a part of our becoming? Through a review process after each death, do we resolve to do better in our next life? Ian Stevenson, M.D., Carlson Professor of Psychiatry and Director of the Division of Personality Studies at the University of Virginia, undertook the task to gather and investigate some 3,000 cases of reported reincarnation. His colleague, Jim B. Tucker, in *Life Before Life*, reports on a number of these cases and offers striking evidence that verifies the stories that Stevenson collected. Carol Bowman, in *Children's Past Lives*, records remarkable stories of children who remember a past life. Characteristically, these reports are of individuals whose lives—through accidents, war or illness—were cut short abruptly as children or as young adults. Such traumatic events in a former life apparently manifest in the present life as a phobia—an unreasonable fear of fire or water or loud noises, often too, night terrors. Apparently the child is experiencing the past trauma as though he or she were still living the former life. Many of these children, it appears, have reincarnated rather quickly and are able to locate people, still living, with whom they lived in their former life. While many of them report no memory of an in-between state, there are those who speak of a 'heaven' experience before their return to physical life.

One of these stories is that of James Leininger, a young boy who remembers his former life, in which he died as a fighter pilot in World War II. His story is recorded in the book *Soul Survivor*, as reported by his parents, Andrea and Bruce Leininger. The Leiningers recount that four-year-old James, having just received his third G.I. Joe action figure from Santa, was asked by his Dad:

> "So what are you going to name your new G.I. Joe, James?"
> "Walter."
> "Hey, how come you named your G.I. Joes Billy and Leon and Walter?"
> "Because that's who met me when I got to heaven."

It was later established that Billy, Leon and Walter, his three fighter pilot friends, had preceded James Huston in death in World War II in battles leading up to the one at Chi-Chijima where James Huston was killed. Other references to a heaven experience may be found in the remarkable stories recorded by Carol Bowman in her book *Return from Heaven*.

Turning to religion, though Hinduism, Buddhism, and

other Eastern religions teach the concepts of reincarnation and karma, mainstream Islam, Judaism, and Christianity do not. It is worth noting, however, that Elaine Pagels, Ph.D., in *The Gnostic Gospels*, states that these concepts were current and accepted at the time of Christ. They are certainly implied in the story of "The Man Born Blind" (John 9:1-41) when the disciples ask Jesus, "Who sinned, this man or his parents, that he was born blind?" The question clearly implies the possibility of both a past life and of karma. Jesus does not chide them for asking a foolish question. He simply tells them that in this case there is a different answer. If we consider the import of the question, however, we can realize that if the man's blindness was the karmic result of a sin, it could only have happened in a former life. Clearly, to the disciples and to Jesus, it was a perfectly reasonable question to ask.

Each of the three monotheistic religions—Islam, Judaism, and Christianity—does have an esoteric side that teaches the concepts of reincarnation and karma. Islam has Sufism and Judaism has the Kabbalah. In the Christian tradition, the esoteric stream that teaches these principles, once a part of the early Church, reappears in the teachings of Anthroposophy and in The Christian Community: Movement for Religious Renewal.

If reincarnation and karma are realities, do they help us make sense of life? Looking at the different destinies of people it can be hard to believe in a God of love. Some of us are well clothed, well fed, well educated, while others are starving, illiterate, or mentally or physically handicapped. One life? The possibility of multiple lives can help make sense of this conundrum. Walt Whitman's poem "Faces" sets this troubling contradiction into poetic form, as the poet realizes that even the poorest wretch before him will appear "perfect and unharm'd" when he comes back in another life to look upon his face again.

Investigations into this spiritual realm that children intimate and poets describe have attracted many mystics, thinkers, and philosophers. Rudolf Steiner (1861-1925)—philosopher, educator, scientist, and artist—provides us, through his spiritual research, with a picture of what happens to the soul after death, its sojourn in the spiritual world—a world of beings—and its preparation for the new life. The review process after death he speaks of is something we find corroborated in reports of people who have had near death experiences. Raymond Moody, M.D., in *Life After Life* and *The Light Beyond*, describes many of these experiences and how people who have been declared clinically dead, and then resuscitated, report seeing their lives unfold before them. This review takes place in the company of a "Being of Light," a loving and non-judgmental presence, which people describe variously as an angel, or as God, or as Christ. The soul experiences all the events of the life just lived and the ramifications of all its deeds. The soul also lives through all of its interactions with others from the other person's point of view. This experience is what generates the desire in the soul to make good in a future life all in which it fell short in this life, and gives it the impetus to return. We understand, and therefore we judge ourselves. Most people who have had a near death experience report that their subsequent lives are completely changed and that they have no fear of death.

Is it our task in these times to unite the two sides of the threshold—to move from belief to experience? This collection of writings could perhaps encourage us to move imaginatively in that direction. Rumi calls to us—"Don't go back to sleep," and points to "where the two worlds touch."

The question may be asked about the aspect of forgetting—both our former lives and our life in the spiritual world before birth. Most of us have completely forgotten, so when young children speak of these things we may not listen carefully or take them seriously. Perhaps this book will encourage a new openness in parents and a respect for the mature soul in their care, struggling to penetrate its little body, and to acquire the language of earth with which to express its remembrance of heaven.

Books of Interest

Bauer, Dietrich, Max Hoffmeister, and Hartmut Goerg. *Children Who Communicate Before They are Born: Conversations with Unborn Souls*. Forest Row, England: Temple Lodge, 2005 (English). Verlag Urachhaus (German), 1986.

Bowman, Carol. *Children's Past Lives: How Past Life Memories Affect Your Child*. New York: Bantam Books, 1997.

Bowman, Carol. *Return from Heaven: Beloved Relatives Reincarnated Within Your Family*. New York: Harper Torch, 2001.

Carman, Elizabeth M. and Neil J. Carman. *Cosmic Cradle: Souls Waiting in the Wings for Birth*. Fairfield, Iowa: Sunstar Publishing, 1999.

Chamberlain, David. *Babies remember birth: and other extraordinary scientific discoveries about the mind and personality of your newborn*. Los Angeles : J.P. Tarcher, 1988. Later published as *The Mind of Your Newborn Baby*, North Atlantic Books, 1998.

Coudris, Manuel David. *Diary of an Unborn Child: An Unborn Baby Speaks to its Mother*. Bath, England: Gateway Books, 1992. (Original work published in German, 1985.)

Gabriel, Michael and Marie Gabriel. *Remembering Your Life Before Birth: How Your Womb Memories Have Shaped Your Life – And How to Heal Them*. Santa Rosa, California: Aslan, 1992.

Hallett, Elisabeth. *Soul Trek: Meeting Our Children on the Way to Birth. Stories of the Unborn Soul: The Mystery and Delight of Pre-Birth Communication*. Bloomington, Indiana: iUniverse, 2002.

Heinz, Sarah. *Coming from the Light, Spiritual Accounts of Life Before Life*. New York: Pocket Books, 1997. (Original work published 1994.)

Klaus, Marshall and Phyllis Klaus. *Your Amazing Newborn*. Reading, Massachusetts: Perseus Books, 1998. (Original work published 1985.)

Leininger, Andrea and Bruce Leininger. *Soul Survivor: The Reincarnation of a World War II Fighter Pilot*. New York: Grand Central Publishing, 2009.

Luminare-Rosen, Carista. *Parenting Begins Before Conception: A Guide to Preparing Body, Mind and Spirit for You and Your Future Child*. Rochester, Vermont: Healing Press Arts, 2000.

McManus, Mary Grace. *Cheyenne: Journey to Birth*. Lynwood, Washington: Clay Mountain Press, 1999.

Mills, Roy. *The Soul's Remembrance: Earth is Not Our Home*. Seattle, Washington: Onjinjinkta, 1999.

Moody, Raymond A. *Life After Life*. Covington, Georgia: Mockingbird Books, 1975.

Moody, Raymond A. *The Light Beyond*. New York: HarperCollins, 1975, 2001.

Salter, Joan. *The Incarnating Child*. UK: Hawthorne Press, 1987.

Schwartz, Howard. *Before You Were Born*. Brookfield, Connecticut: Roaring Brook Press, 2005.

Selg, Peter. *Unborness*. Great Barrington, Massachusetts: Steiner Books, 2010.

Szejer, Myriam. *Des Mots Pour Naitre (Words to be Born: Psychoanalytic Listening in the Maternity Unit)*. Paris, France: Gallimard, 1997.

Van der Wal, Jaap. <www.embryo.nl.> *See also* YouTube, "Embryo in Motion."

Verny, Thomas, and John Kelly. *The Secret Life of the Unborn Child*. New York: Dell, 1986.

Wade, Jenny. *Changes of Mind: A Holonomic Theory of the Evolution of Consciousness*. Albany, New York: State University of New York Press, 1996.

Wambach, Helen. *Life Before Life*. New York: Bantam Books, 1979.

Weiss, Brian L. *Many Lives, Many Masters: The True Story of a Prominent Psychiatrist, His Young Patient, and the Past-Life Therapy that Changed Both Their Lives*. New York: Simon and Schuster, 1985.

Widdison, Harold. *Trailing Clouds of Glory*. Springville, Utah: Cedar Fort Inc., 2004.

Wilder, Thornton. *Nascuntur Poetae...*, in *The Collected Short Plays of Thornton Wilder Volume 2*. New York: Theater Communications Group, 1998.

Permissions and Sources

Our thanks are due to the authors, or their representatives and the publishers concerned, for permission to include poems and prose excerpts from works under copyright, as noted below.

Al-Ghazali: "Know that we are not Created," from *The Alchemy of Happiness*, translated by Claud Field. London: J. Murray, 1909.

David Axelrod: "Near Death," from *Random Beauty* by David B. Axelrod. Copyright © 2001 American House. By permission of the author.

Christy Barnes: "Bumble Baby" and "Unborn Child," from *A Wound Awoke Me* by Christy Barnes. Copyright © 1994 Adonis Press. Used by permission of Adonis Press.

Alfred Baur, PhD: "A Different Moon – Grave and Gay." Copyright © 1995, reprinted by kind permission of his wife Dr. med. Ilse Baur.

Laurence Binyon: "Unsated Memory," from *Collected Poems*, MacMillan & Co. Ltd., 1931.

Marion Cornish: "To the Unborn," from *A Half Century's Verse*. Copyright © 1973 F.J.C. Cornish. Made and printed by Strange the Printer, Ltd, Sussex, England.

Arvia MacKaye Ege: "For a Newborn Child" and "O My Angel," from *The Secret Iron of the Heart: Songs at the Forge of Awakening Man* by Arvia MacKaye Ege. Copyright © 1982 Adonis Press. Used by permission of Adonis Press.

The Forgotten Books of Eden, edited by Rutherford H. Platt, Jr. Cleveland: W. Collins & World Pub. Co., 1927.

translation by Matthew Barton, published in *Unbornness*, copyright © 2010 Peter Selg, published by SteinerBooks, translated by Margot M. Saar. *Unbornness* was originally published in German by Verlag Ita Wegman Instituts, 2009, as *Ungeborenheit. Die Praëexistenz des Menschen und der Weg zur Gebort*. Reprinted by permission of Matthew Barton.

Joan Salter: "Meditation for Mothers" by the late Joan Salter, from *The Incarnating Child* by Joan Salter, used by permission from the publisher, Hawthorn Press Ltd, UK. <http://www.hawthornpress.com>

Howard Schwartz: "The Angel of Conception," from *Gabriel's Palace: Jewish Mystical Tales* by Howard Schwartz, Oxford University Press, 1993. Copyright © Howard Schwartz. Reprinted by permission of Oxford University Press and Howard Schwartz.

Ina Seidel: "Annunciation," from *Children Who Communicate Before They Are Born*. Temple Lodge, 2005. Originally published in German under the title *Gespräche mit Ungeborenen, Kinder kündigen sich an*, Verlag Urachhaus, 1986. English translation by Pauline Wehrle. Reprinted by permission of Temple Lodge.

Stephen Spender: "I Think Continually of Those," from *New Collected Poems*, by Stephen Spender. Copyright © 2004, reprinted by kind permission of the Estate of Stephen Spender and Ed Victor Ltd.

Elizabeth Spires: "Worlding," "The Summer of Celia," and "Celia Dreaming," from Worldling. Copyright © 1995, used by permission of W.W. Norton and Company, Inc., New York.

Jon Stallworthy: "The Almond Tree" and "The Firstborn," from *Rounding the Horn: Collected Poems*. Copyright © 1998 Carcanet Press, UK. Used by permission of Carcanet Press.

Van Waffle: "Made in Secret," from *Stories of the Unborn Soul: The Mystery and Delight of Pre-Birth Communication* by Elisabeth Hallett, iUniverse. Copyright © 2002 Van Waffle. Reprinted with kind permission from Van Waffle and Elisabeth Hallett.

Jaap van der Wal: "Conception" by Jaap van der Wal, MD: Embryologist, phenomenologist, and initiator of the project *Embryo in Motion*. <http://www.embryo.nl> Translated by Annelies Davidson. Reprinted by permission of the author and the translator.

Thornton Wilder: "Nascuntur Poetae . . ." from *The Collected Short Plays of Thornton Wilder, (Vol II)*, Theater Communications Group, 1998. First published as "The Walled City" in the Yale Literary Magazine, 1918. This work is in the public domain. Additional information about Thornton Wilder may be found at <http://www.thorntonwilder.com>

This volume contains previously unpublished stories and poems for which permission has been granted by the authors. All authors retain copyright to their material: Alisa N. Hackl-Weiss, Hélène Besnard, Martha Loving Orgain, Roger Schultz, Tia Hall, Nancy Holt, Susan Howard, Mark Hulbert, Jo Anne Jeffries, Janet Klaar, Ann Lang, Robin Lawton, Mary Beth Mueller, Janni Nicol, Aileen Niessen, Robin Olson, Janet Parsons.

Index of Authors

Index of First Lines

First lines of stories are in *italics*.

Acknowledgements

My thanks are due to many people over many years who helped this collection come into being. First the contributors, whose inspired writings are the bedrock of this book. Then come the many friends and acquaintances who helped to send me on this remarkable journey by pointing me towards relevant poets, poems, stories, and scriptures. The diligence and cooperation of reference librarians at Duke University, the University of North Carolina, and the Rudolf Steiner Library are also deeply appreciated.

Sincere thanks are due to Tia Hall for her patience and computer skills in typing the manuscript, finding copyright permission information, and keeping track of permission requests. Susan Olive gave generously of her time and professional talents with regard to copyright matters. As the book neared completion my sister, Robin Lawton, lent her considerable editorial skills to the project. Her warmth and enthusiasm for what was coming into being have been an incredible gift.

Working with my editor, Maurice York, at Wrightwood Press has been an entirely positive experience. His ear for language and his aesthetic sense have added greatly to the work.

For Bruce and Kathryn who brought Lily, our first grandchild, into the world, and whose coming inspired this book – thank you.

Last, but not least, I would like to honor Bill, my beloved husband of more than forty years. His encouragement of the work, as well as his forbearance and patience with a rather distracted wife—and many a late meal—are deeply appreciated.

About the Editor

Eve Olive was born in Tennessee but grew up in South Africa from the age of three. She has a Degree in Architecture from the University of Natal in Durban. Her second profession is eurythmy, which she studied in Switzerland and New York. Eurythmy is an art of movement that uses the body to express the gestures inherent in the sound of language and music. Poems can be performed; the audible can be made visible. Eve taught for many years at the Emerson Waldorf School in Chapel Hill, NC, which she helped to found and design. Her adult eurythmy classes have been ongoing since 1975 and have given rise to several performances, notably "Prayers from the Ark," "The Creation Myth of the Cherokee Indian," and "The Creation Myth of the Yoruba." Eve lives with her husband in a one-hundred-year-old farmhouse in Orange County, North Carolina.